A Way Out of No Way

Harlem Prep: Transforming Dropouts into Scholars, 1967-1977

By

Dr. Hussein Ah

and

Hillary Chapman

With Love,
Hussein
NYC, 2016

A Way Out of No Way

Harlem Prep: Transforming Dropouts into Scholars,

1967-1977

By Dr. Hussein Ahdieh & Hillary Chapman

Publisher: CreateSpace, an Amazon Company

Available through Amazon.com and other channels

Dedication

This book is dedicated to all the teachers, students, and benefactors who made the Prep a reality and helped the lives of so many young people. I especially remember my late Baha'i friends Alvin Burley, Ann Carpenter, Ed Carpenter, John Czerniejewski, and Mae Morgan, who served at Harlem Prep, and the late Judge Robert Mangum who cared deeply about its success.

Hussein Ahdieh

Also by Hussein Ahdieh & Hillary Chapman
Available through Amazon.com and other booksellers

Awakening: A History of the Bahá'í and Bábí Faiths in Nayriz

Awakening describes the tumultuous birth of the Bábí movement in Nayriz and its later evolution into that city's Bahá'í community. It recounts the heroic struggles of the Bábís in 1850 and 1853 against the overwhelming forces of Iran's despotic monarchy and the horrific treatment of the survivors. It covers in depth the story of Vahíd – a practical as well as spiritual leader. The book also provides an account of the less-known but dramatic upheaval of 1909. Awakening is a story of ordinary people transforming themselves into heroes and heroines through the empowering Message brought by the Báb and Bahá'u'lláh. Website: AwakeningNayriz.org

'Abdu'l-Bahá in New York

Of all the historical, religious and cultural events in the history of the United States, the arrival of 'Abdu'l-Bahá in 1912 was the most important one of all. Many people—from all facets of society—had the honor to meet Him, attend His talks, benefit from His wisdom and witness His benevolence and humility. Their encounters with Him were life-altering: He touched the depths of their souls and awakened them spiritually. This re-telling of 'Abdu'l-Bahá's days in New York City will bring you closer to this unique figure in spiritual history, whose life will serve as a model of the true spiritual and ethical life for centuries to come. Website: AbdulBahaInNewYork.org

The Calling: Tahirih of Persia and her American Contemporaries
(Available Soon)

This book introduces Tahirih of Qazvin (a female mystic and poet in 19th century Persia) to an American audience. A free-spirited harbinger of women's rights, Tahirih stood in the forefront of the one of the most powerful religious movements to emerge in Persia and the Near East during the 19th century—the Babi Faith. This highly readable and carefully researched account tells the little-known story of her extraordinary life in the context of the Persian Shi'a Muslim world in which she moved. This engaging narrative is interlaced with intimate accounts of the courageous lives of great American female figures from the Great Awakenings. Though half a world away, these women shared a *zeitgeist* with Tahirih.
Website: TahirihThePureOne.com

Table of Contents

Introduction

What does an educational experiment from almost a half-century ago have to do with today?

The Harlem Preparatory School was founded in 1967 for the purpose of preparing dropouts in central Harlem for college and careers, and to take their places in society as well-informed citizens. These were often teenagers for whom an indifferent public school system held no interest and who were struggling with family or community challenges. Through the concerted efforts of teachers, administrators, supporters, and the students themselves, Harlem Prep proved that these youth could achieve academic success and go on to higher education.

Today's troubling reality is that a larger number of youth live in poverty than ever before. Poor neighborhoods still have poor public schools that limit the possibilities of its children. The dropout rate among minorities is high, and their academic achievement lags behind that of their more affluent counterparts. Many cities continue to have deep pockets of poverty including a seemingly permanent black urban underclass. Race, poverty, and educational failure often still seem to go hand in hand.

Do we need a kickstarter educational effort to lift our young people out of poverty, ignorance, and lack of opportunity? Harlem Prep shows us that this can be done if there are valid educational concepts, motivated students, and faculty and administrators who can think outside of the box and are supported by sustained funding.

I immigrated to the United States over fifty years ago from Iran to seek educational and economic opportunity and to flee religious persecution where the Baha'i Faith, my religion, is reviled by the Muslim clergy and their fundamentalist followers. The memory of being a second-class citizen helped me to empathize with black Americans faced with white racism. Even as a new immigrant, I could see the effects of long-term racism on the lives of many black

Americans who so often seemed trapped in menial work and segregated into sub-standard housing and neighborhoods.

I became involved with Harlem Prep through my friendship with Ann and Ed Carpenter whom I knew through the Baha'i community. Ed had been appointed the headmaster of a new school, a "free school", whose purpose was to prepare former 'dropouts' for college. I was still a student at university myself, and I eagerly contributed ideas during the conceptualization phase. When I completed my bachelor's degree, I joined the faculty of Harlem Prep as a math teacher and from there moved into the role of assistant headmaster. I can say unequivocally that it was the most satisfying and purposeful job in my entire education career. While serving full time as an administrator, I was able to complete my doctoral degree in education at the University of Massachusetts focusing on alternative schools with Harlem Prep as a prototype.

One scene summarizes why I was at Harlem Prep. An unwed teenage mother visited my office with her baby and her mother, whom I doubt was much over thirty. Standing in front of me was the potential for either another family in a generation that would grow up in poverty or for a breakout life of accomplishment and fulfillment. Harlem Prep provided the way forward for this young woman and many more students such as Janet MacDonald who went from humble beginnings in Brooklyn to becoming an award-winning writer of children's books and a resident of France. I am proud and grateful to have been part of Harlem Prep's contribution to the lives of so many young people.

This book reconstructs the history of Harlem Prep through the stories and challenges of those who made the schools a reality— founders, funders, teachers, administrators, and students, and the newspaper and journal articles that reported on this important project.

If you are a Harlem Prep alumni or faculty, I hope you enjoy these memories.

If you are an educator, teacher, or someone involved in a "free school" or charter school, I hope this account inspires you to continue your important service.

If you are a campaigner against multigenerational poverty, I invite you to examine how we tried to help those young people least likely to succeed.

Many people have contributed their time, talent, and money, toward the success of the school. I would like to thank all of the teachers, students, parents, and individuals who were a part of Harlem Prep, including: Sandy George Campbell, Elizabeth McLoughlin, Sheila Mosler, Harvey Spears, Frank Shea, Congressman Charles Rangel, Dr. Josh Smith, and Dr. William Smith. In addition, I am grateful for the devotion of Tatiana Jordan and Robert Hanevold to this book.

Hussein Ahdieh   New York City, February, 2015

Prologue

Afros in the sun, gleaming white hair, black and white men in business attire and women in pleated skirts, a young Catholic priest back by the fence, one nun among the students, another in front of the graduates who are all dressed in formal blue blazers with the logo "Moja Logo"—the community and the teachers are graduating the Harlem Prep Class of '69.

The years of Mao and Che, Paris and Prague, the Panthers and the Underground, civil rights and race riots, LSD-free-love-mind-alteration, miniskirts, abortion rights, Woodstock, Jimi, Sly, James, black and proud, the fight against poverty, "The times they are a changin'", are peaking.

The ceremony is being held out on 136th street a few feet from the corner of Eighth Ave., in central Harlem, an expression of the highest aspirations of this struggling neighborhood and the lives of these young people and their families.

Down on the corner a long Oldsmobile sits with its trunk popped open under the large letters BAR MAX'S CAFÉ. A man leans against the outside of the bar, another is crossing the street. A WNYC television van waits next to the large group to report this community victory.

The bullhorn speaker amplifies the reading of the Pledge of Allegiance as the students and audience place their hands over their hearts. The ceremony unfolds. The young nun beams as she hands a diploma to a student. Each graduate will be attending college. Some are the first in their families to do so, many were considered beyond redemption.

Everyone stands close together, adults facing the young people whom they have nurtured into taking the next step in their lives—college—towards a more fulfilling life, a broader freedom, mental enlightenment, a surer sense of justice.

There was a viable way forward.

1 ~ Saying "No" to the Downward Spiral

Gene Callender knew nothing of the baby dish, the silver comb, the brush, the silver spoon, that his grandmother in Barbados had sent him when he was born in far away New York City. His father had kept them in a trunk containing objects from a poverty-stricken past he had left behind to emigrate to the United States, but the memory of which he could not let go of completely. He was a tough man who took the Biblical instruction not spare the rod seriously and regularly beat his boy. He also worked very hard and took pride in having been a chauffeur in Barbados—a high status job there-and kept his chauffeur's cap in his room all his life, insisting that—whatever menial work he happened to be doing at the time—he was a chauffeur.

After his mother's death, Gene found letters that his mother had exchanged with her family over the years; in one his grandmother had written, "Kiss the baby for me". His mother had come to the United States from Barbados to work as live-in help and send money back home. She read her Bible studiously and passionately, and served her friends and neighbors selflessly. Conscious of her color in this new country, she disliked the dark skin tone of her little boy and incessantly applied cream on his skin hoping to lighten it.

The Callender family settled in a Cambridge, Massachusetts, a neighborhood made up of immigrants who all struggled together to make it in this new country. Here was a multi-racial cultural fabric that supported everyone. Gene retained a great love for Greek food from eating it in his boyhood friend's home.

But beyond this island of multi-racial understanding, the reality of the United States showed Gene that he was often unwelcome. While on an errand for his father, the owner of the Stop and Shop accused him of trying to steal a can of tuna. His father brought Gene back to store and shouted at the frightened owner that his son was not a thief. Everyone was terrified but Gene remembers this as a time when he felt very connected to his father.[1]

Gene learned of Harlem from his alcoholic uncle Fred, whom the family made live in the unheated attic of the house to convey their moral disapproval of his dissolute life. Fred had given him *New World A Coming: Inside Black America* by Roi Ottley, from which he learned of Harlem and its "black aristocracy" and read to him from black owned publications *The Afro-American Newspaper* and *The Pittsburgh Courier.* At this stage, the young Gene Callender began to picture himself becoming the kind of leader that emerged from these pages.[2]

In the Harlem of 1944, he found a place with multitudes of black people, something he had never seen before. Their inter-connected families were bound together into a strong community characterized by love and trust.

Peter had followed his older brother out of the New York City public school system and into Ryker's prison. He also discovered the poetry of ee cummings and Shelley, whose verses he would say aloud, and the Harlem Prep school, which he read about in an ad placed in a magazine by the ESSO oil company:

> *'The high school where every graduate goes to college.*
>
> *Harlem Prep is less than three years old. It has its home in an old supermarket. There is no other independent school in America quite like it.*
>
> *It is a school for dropouts. It confronts these dropouts with quite a challenge. You can't get a diploma from Harlem Prep until you are accepted by a college.*
>
> *So far, 110 students have been graduated and have entered college. None has failed or dropped out.*
>
> *Some record.*
>
> *When you visit Harlem Prep, you get an inkling of what makes it tick. There are no walls between classrooms. And almost no walls between minds. Teachers don't just lecture. Students don't just listen. They argue. They laugh. And sometimes you hear a burst of good, healthy anger.*
>
> *Ed Carpenter, the headmaster, doesn't pretend that his school has all the answers. Far from it. But he does believe that it is providing a small haven of good sense where religions and races, students and teachers can get together and learn from one another. Then reach their own conclusions.*

Clearly, a great deal can be learned from an experimental school like Harlem Prep. Its good work must continue. This takes support. Jersey Standard is proud to have provided some of it."

○

"Jesus is the doctor, Services on Sunday" read the sign over the church door. In 1926, 140 churches sanctified a 150-block area of Harlem. Two thirds of these churches were storefront or home churches—such as "The Metaphysical Church of the Divine Investigation", the "Sanctified Sons of the Holy Ghost", and the "Live-Ever-Die-Never"—which fed the spiritual needs of tens of thousands of black migrants who had made their way from the rural Carolinas and Virginia to the streets of Harlem, the 'Black Mecca'.[3]

Half a century before, Harlem had been a suburb of New York City. The elevator train came up to Harlem between 1878-1881, and large gracious homes with many spacious rooms rose up from the 1870s to the 1890s. Electricity lit up Harlem in 1887, and the telephone came the following year. The white families in these homes brought black servants and other help with them, and a small black community grew there. This real estate boom went bust in 1905, and prices fell. This allowed large numbers of black New Yorkers to move up into Harlem, aided by black realtors; one especially rich one was known as the "father of Colored Harlem".[4]

The majority of the black residents of Harlem in 1910 had fled the South in the previous decades. The protections of the Reconstruction period had collapsed there and given way to an aggressive and oppressive white supremacy. More black Americans were lynched, tortured, and disenfranchised in the decades of the 1880s-1900s than in any other previous period of American history. No wonder the American Colonization Society which had helped found the country of Liberia with ex-slaves and populate Serra Leone was revived. In 1917, the largest black public demonstration, the "Silent Parade", took place in New York City to protest the killing of over two hundred black Americans by white mobs in St Louis and to demand that President Wilson make good on his promise to enact and enforce anti-lynching laws, which he never did. So with these frightening realities in the South and the lure of jobs with the growing industries in the North, new generations of Southern black Americans were willing to give up the soil for the city.[5]

During these turn of the century decades, black Harlemites made steady gains with the emergence of several black public schools, black civic officials, and organizations such as the NAACP as well as the National League for Urban Conditions, and the move from downtown of virtually every major black institution. The black church, the most stable institution in the area, invested heavily in real estate as did black realtors from other American cities

By 1920, two-thirds of all black New Yorkers lived in Harlem. This decade would see a "New Negro Movement" later known as the "Harlem Renaissance", a flowering of black culture and thought and one of the cultural high water marks in the nation's history. WEB DuBois, among the most influential of all black American intellectuals and author of the seminal *The Souls of Black* Folk, had long advocated for the rights and protections of black people and for equality through integration. He documented and denounced the frequent killings of black Americans during the early decades of the century. During the Harlem Renaissance, he encouraged new black arts and artists, but he believed that art should be used to advance the political and social position of black Americans. Another great intellectual, Alain Locke, contributed to and edited a landmark book of black American literature, *The New Negro*, in 1925. He encouraged black people to be self-confident and politically aware and to cease compromising with the indignities heaped upon them by white people. Locke was also an early member of the Baha'i Faith, a new world religion.

During this Harlem Renaissance, plays appeared on the stage which rejected minstrel stereotypes and presented black actors demonstrating the full range of human emotion. Politically challenging poetry, essays, and articles were published with many forms of new thought, including criticisms of Christianity and established ways. The piano—the instrument of the wealthy—and the new "stride style" was incorporated into the popular brass bands, and jazz music began to broaden and become more sophisticated. In these and other fields, all racial stereotypes and limitations imposed on black Americans were challenged; this dynamic and complex cultural flourishing made a way for future generations of great black American artists and thinkers.

At the same time, though, the 1920s marked the decline of Harlem from a stable middle class neighborhood into a slum marred by the problems of poverty. Tens of thousands of black migrants from the rural south moved there to get their share in the Promise Land. James

Weldon Johnson spoke of Harlem as becoming the "the greatest Negro city in the world".[6] During this decade, 89,417 black people moved to Harlem mostly from the South, and 118,792 white immigrant Harlemites moved to the outer boroughs and beyond. Moving "up" out of the old neighborhood was a common pattern for second and third generation immigrants but was not the pattern that was followed by black Americans because racial discrimination prevented them from finding housing in other areas with the same ease as their white counterparts. The high demand for housing drove up the rents, but the new black migrants from the South could ill-afford these, much less maintain or develop the properties. Rents doubled between 1919 and 1927; the average black person in Harlem paid $9.50 in rent whereas the average white middle-class renter in New York City paid 6.67$. The combination of high rents and low wages meant that rooms were crowded. Well-paying work was difficult to come by for these new arrivals; a prominent sociologist noted that there were two kinds of jobs for black people, "Those that employ negroes in menial positions and those that employ no negroes at all."[7] The new migrants had small families and modest means, and they needed small affordable apartments; most of Harlem's buildings to homes and apartments, though, were built before 1900 and had large, expensive rooms—so tenants were packed in. Harlem had the highest population density of most any area in the United States; there were 336 persons living per square acre in Harlem compared to 223 per square acre in other parts of New York City.[8]

Conflict between tenants and landlords—both black and white— were rife; the Harlem District Court was the busiest in the city. Conditions in the buildings deteriorated as landlords increasingly lost interest in maintenance. Many of the migrants had come from poverty stricken rural areas and had neither the experience nor the means to upkeep the properties they were renting. Rats, refuse, damage to property, all proliferated. So did diseases such as rickets caused by poor nutrition. Many houses of prostitution—mostly owned by whites—, and dens for gambling gobbled up hard-earned dollars.[9] A "wild west" atmosphere developed in Harlem, both of opportunity and of degradation. Crime and delinquency jumped. All of these inter-related complex problems opened the way for the flood of narcotics that came into Harlem, and city leaders were not prepared to make the broad structural changes required to reverse this decline.

When Bradley finished grade school, her mother started to fade from her life so she had to grow up very quickly. Her mother had been strict but now she had almost no supervision—or support—at all. She knew she would have to make her own way. She spent many hours on the streets. She visited churches and centers. She was alone most of the time. She wanted a place where she could find guidance, structure, and a path to college and a future. She signed up to take the entrance test for the Harlem Prep School.

Whitney Young fondly remembered walking the railroad tracks between Louisville and Nashville while his father recounted family stories. He loved planting the family garden and playing croquet and baseball in the yard. His was a sheltered life on the rural Kentucky campus of Lincoln Institute which his father headed. In his father Whitney saw a black man who administered a staff of both black and white teachers working harmoniously together. His father could honor the rules of the white man without giving up his own dignity. His mother showed a more freewheeling spirit as she drank at the WHITE ONLY water fountain and used the WHITE ONLY restrooms when going about their business in their small Kentucky town.[10]

Young's ability to move in two worlds worked well for him in adulthood. An early black American colleague at the Urban League described him as "the kind of guy that I think would impress whites".[11] His secretary remembered that "he could relate to the business world as well as the man on the street".[12] This made him effective in his work of improving the economic lot of black Americans during his time in the Urban League of Omaha, Nebraska.[13] His appointment in the 1950s as Dean of the School of Social Work in Atlanta brought him into direct contact with the emerging Civil Rights Movement that would sweep the country.

With the collapse of Reconstruction and the passing of innumerable local Jim Crow laws, the civil rights gains of black Americans in the post-Civil War era were all but erased. Nearly a century would crawl by before a national civil rights awakening would begin in the 1950s. Genuinely popular, democratic, and diverse, the Civil Rights Movement emerged—initially with protests against a few of the countless daily indignities endured by black Americans that reflected the much deeper, broader, and more sinister views held by too many white Americans. Through bus boycotts, sit-ins, and marches guided by a philosophy of non-violent civil disobedience broadcast over the young media of television, this movement caught the attention of the nation and of a rising generation interested in social change to become a national movement that focused on the enactment of laws and their enforcement.

During this dynamic period Whitney Young was appointed, in 1960, to head the National Urban League, which had the mission of improving the social and economic position of black Americans through inter-racial teamwork.[14] Such a mission was tailor-made for a man with Young's upbringing. The Urban League had been in existence for much of the century but had fallen into the doldrums, and he was hired to infuse it with socially relevant vigor. Under him, the League challenged the constant attempts to thwart the legal advances that had been made in civil rights and to remedy the competitive disadvantage faced by blacks because of the legacy of racism. He noted that "it is one thing to eliminate barriers; it is another to get effective utilization of the new resources."[15] In furthering the aims of the Urban League, Whitney Young worked with black civil rights leaders and white business and governmental leaders—including the President of the United States. He was the lone black American on a trip of several CEOs of Fortune 500 companies to Eastern Europe, one of who noted that "if more Negroes were like you there wouldn't be any problem", to which he responded, "if more white people were like me there wouldn't be any problem". Henry Ford II became enamored of him. After a flight, he carried Young's briefcase off the plane, which the press noted. Young liked to reminisce that Henry Ford had been his bag carrier. His intelligence, charisma, mix of charm and toughness, and willingness to engage with white people won the respect of the CEOs on the trip, a pattern which would characterize his whole public life but which more radical black leaders would denounce.[16]

Among his more significant initiatives for young people would be the establishment of "street academies", alternative schools to help dropouts re-integrate into education and prepare for college. These would have a direct impact in Harlem.

The 1960s saw the consensus of the '50s give way to an idealism that challenged that consensus, driven in large part by the powerful new Civil Rights Movement. For many in this generation, the great post World War II prosperity now had to translate into real social change. This was expressed politically when the Kennedy administration was elected into office in 1960. The political leadership for creating this social change fell unwittingly to the hard-driving, wheeling and dealing Lyndon Johnson who was born and reared in Texas, a state not known for its civil rights ideals. He called for the creation of a "Great Society":

> "We stand at the edge of the greatest era in the life of any nation. For the first time in world history, we have the abundance and the ability to free every man from hopeless want.... This nation ... has man's first chance to create a Great Society ..."[17]

The Great Society was a massive legislative effort to defend and advance civil rights and to alleviate poverty. By the time the 89th Congress had adjourned in October of 1966, one-hundred and eighty-one of the two-hundred major pieces of legislation that had been submitted were enacted.[18] The Federal Government was now an active player in society, engaged in civil rights, poverty, education, health, housing, pollution, the arts, urban development, occupational safety, consumer protection, and mass transit.

The "War on Poverty" involved the creation of numerous programs to address a wide variety of issues related to poverty and work. The public was in a receptive mood as the economy was doing well—take-home pay rose 21% for the middle class.[19] These programs included the Job Corps to train people for work, the Small Business and Rural Loan programs to provide funding, and the very popular Head Start early education program for small children, among many others. In cities, Community Action Agencies were created to empower individuals through participatory democracy at the grass roots level. These ran into real problems as the agencies tussled with the mayors over who controlled the incoming funds. The conflicts grew worse when a new "black power" ideology was fused with the agencies, the business community resisted, and self-serving local politicians angled to benefit financially. The large number of programs combined with hasty planning, and a growing perception among whites that these programs aimed to help only minorities, led to disenchantment with the War on Poverty. This massive effort did not address the needed structural changes in the economy, nor did it create jobs, so people were being trained for jobs that either did not exist or that could not pay enough to lift them out of poverty. Still, the number of poor dropped substantially over the course of the 1960s. The Great Society was the first such large-scale, in-depth examination of poverty, and the closer people looked at it, the more complex its problems appeared.[20] On civil rights, Johnson wanted to continue Kennedy's legacy:

"No memorial oration or eulogy could more eloquently honor President Kennedy's memory than the earliest possible passage of the civil rights bills for which he fought so long. We have talked long enough in this country about equal rights. We have talked for one hundred years or more. It is now time to write the next chapter—and to write it in the book of law."[21]

Johnson's 1964 Civil Rights bill was a second attempt at the 1963 bill which had failed. This second attempt took eighty days of Congressional debate, thousands of pages entered into the Congressional Record, and the longest filibuster in history. One Senator from Illinois, described as the "Wizard of Ooze" who "marinated his tonsils daily with a mixture of Pond's cold cream and water, which he gargled and swallowed"[22] was seen to be the key to its passage. A careful reader of polling, he ended up voting in favor of the bill over the dire warnings of another Senator that "It would have a tremendous impact on what we have called, in happier times, the American way of life"[23] and that it would make "a Czar of the President of the United States and a Rasputin of the Attorney General";[24] after all, "every man of white Caucasian heritage has a perfect right to protect those institutions in his society which allow him the freedom to associate with the people of his own race...".[25] The core sections of the Civil Rights Act attacked the foundation of segregation and discrimination in the South, barring discrimination in public accommodations and federal assistance programs among others.

But many felt that this law only affirmed what was already enunciated in the Constitution of the United States and the Bill of Rights and did not even begin to address current inequities. A big push was begun to pass a voting rights bill in 1965. Throughout the South there had been large-scale disenfranchisement of black voters; most black people were not registered to vote, and pre-conditions were devised to make it difficult for them to do so. The 1965 march on Selma highlighted these discriminatory practices: new voters were required to fill out a sixty-eight question form and polls were open only for two days for them. A group opposed to the bill warned that "if the bill was passed, the South would disappear from the civilized world", and that the bill was a plot to carry out the "original Stalin plan until the time is ripe for revolution for self-determination in the Black Belt".[26] In the decade after the passage of the Voting Rights Act, the number of new voters increased nine-fold. In the summer of '65, Johnson went further:

> "it is not enough just to open the gates of opportunity. All our citizens must have the ability to walk through the gates.... We seek ... not just equality as a right and a theory but equality as a fact and equality as a result."[27]

The development of affirmative action divided white supporters of civil rights—the divide was between removing racial discrimination and ensuring racial equality. At the other end of the racial/political spectrum, a black nationalist pointed out the difference between expectations and present reality, between promises and the power structure:

> "The ghetto is no promised land. There are no jobs to be integrated into. ... The accepted liberal means don't work. The white power structure has no intention of giving up anything without demands, and power yields only to power."[28]

So, as civil rights laws were being passed, race riots broke out in major urban areas. Civil rights workers were murdered. A white mob in Chicago attacked a housing demonstration by black citizens. Black radicalism frightened mainstream white voters. The civil rights consensus was fracturing in the mid-60s. The promise and hope of Civil Rights Movement was giving way to naked racial conflict in urban areas wracked by the challenges of poverty and racism; such was the case of Harlem in the 1960s.

ᑕ

After Harry Smith's parents separated, he became too much for his mother to take care of. He started to play music with various people. He wasn't into school. He was confused about his identity. He was a black boy growing up in white areas of upstate NY and Maine. He moved to in a small town North Carolina to live with his grandmother who worked as a servant and whose home was heated by a pot-belly stove. The little town was segregated. He went to the movies and had to sit upstairs. When he went downstairs to the main level where black customers were not supposed to go, the owner confronted him and slapped him hard. He heard about Harlem Prep from a family friend. One summer when working in Virginia Beach he went up to New Jersey, and there took the test for Harlem Prep.

James Baldwin, the great American writer, remembered the spiritual desolation, social ruin, and bitter isolation of his Harlem:

"... when I turn east on 131st Street and Lenox Avenue, there is first a soda-pop joint, then a shoeshine "parlor," then a grocery store, then a dry cleaners', then the houses. All along the street there are people who watched me grow up, people who grew up with me, people I watched grow up along with my brothers and sisters; and, sometimes in my arms, sometimes underfoot, sometimes at my shoulder—or on it—their children, a riot, a forest of children, who include my nieces and nephews.

"When we reach the end of this long block, we find ourselves on wide, filthy, hostile Fifth Avenue, facing that project which hangs over the avenue like a monument to the folly, and the cowardice, of good intentions. All along the block, for anyone who knows it, are immense human gaps, like craters. ... I am talking principally about the young. What are they doing? Well, some, a minority, are fanatical churchgoers, members of the more extreme of the Holy Roller sects. Many, many more are "moslems," by affiliation or sympathy, that is to say that they are united by nothing more — and nothing less — than a hatred of the white world and all its works. They are present, for example, at every Buy Black street-corner meeting — meetings in which the speaker urges his hearers to cease trading with white men and establish a separate economy. Neither the speaker nor his hearers can possibly do this, of course, since Negroes do not own General Motors or RCA or the A&P ... Many have given up. ... There are those who are simply sitting on their stoops, "stoned," animated for a moment only, and hideously, by the approach of someone who may lend them the money for a "fix." Or by the approach of someone from whom they can purchase it, one of the shrewd ones, on the way to prison or just coming out.

"And the others, who have avoided all of these deaths, get up in the morning and go downtown to meet "the man." They work in the white man's world all day and come home in the evening to this fetid block. They struggle to instill in their children some private sense of honor or dignity which will help the child to survive. This means, of course, that they must struggle, stolidly, incessantly, to keep this sense alive in themselves, in spite of the insults, the indifference, and the cruelty they are certain to encounter in their working day. ..."

"One remembers them from another time — playing handball in the playground, going to church, wondering if they were going to be promoted at school. One remembers them going off to war — gladly, to escape this block. One remembers their return. ...

"I tried to explain what *has* happened, unfailingly, whenever a significant body of Negroes move North. They do not escape Jim Crow: they merely encounter another, not-less-deadly variety. They do not move to Chicago, they move to the South Side; they do note move to New York, they move to Harlem. The pressure within the ghetto causes the ghetto walls to expand, and this expansion is always violent."[29]

The seething discontent in the ghetto described by James Baldwin exploded in the July heat of 1964 when a fifteen year old black boy was shot and killed by an off-duty white police officer following a minor altercation involving several black youth and a white building superintendent in front of an apartment building. News of the shooting spread fast to a nearby school whose principal informed the students of the incident. Three-hundred students left to protest. The shooting set off six nights of looting and vandalism with over one-hundred people injured and several hundred arrested. Similar rioting erupted in other American cities.[30] These were the worst race riots in Harlem since 1942, when a white police officer shot and killed a black man who was a soldier just returned from World War II. His death came to symbolize the racism faced by even those black Americans who defended the nation in war, and the police officer became the symbol of the ongoing white oppression of the freedoms of black Americans.[31]

Robert Mangum became one of the first high-ranking officials in the New York City Police Department in the 1950s. He had earned a Law degree from Brooklyn College and worked as a patrolman on the streets of New York at the same time.

A large crowd gathered outside the 28th Precinct to protest police violence and demand to see a man who had been injured and taken into custody. Several white officials representing the police department met with the editor of the Amsterdam News, Harlem's leading newspaper, and invited Malcolm X who had great influence over people in the area. The meeting did not go well as Malcom X thought the police were being dismissive, and when he addressed Robert Mangum, according to a police source, was: " ... I don't talk with white man's niggers." Mangum, one source said, was "very hurt". Nevertheless, Malcom X's uncompromising arguments swayed the others and the situation was addressed and diffused.

Later, Malcolm X came into contact with the Baha'i Faith. He hired Frank Sawyer, the first black-owned print shop on 125th Street for print jobs. Sawyer was a Baha'i and invited the famous community figure to attend Baha'i meetings in his home. [32]

Robert Mangum went on to a distinguished career in civil service. He had been appointed first deputy Commissioner of Hospitals, and, later, Commissioner on the New York State Division of Human Rights. By the 1970s, he was a judge in the New York Court of Claims. [33]

Over the course of his career, he was often the only black man at his level of responsibility and seniority. He was the rare black man in those days to be inside the white power structure, but he had to contend both with white racism and the criticism of more radical black leaders who saw his 'insider' status as a compromise. He never ceased to work for the advancement of black Americans. When Harlem Prep went into financial crisis, he worked hard to save it.

James Baldwin's powerful description of Harlem offended some of Harlem's middle class residents, especially his bleak description of the Riverton Development, a prized apartment complex. While the development was not a slum, it was part of the "ghetto"—defined as an area isolated by race—in that Riverton had been built because apartments in Stuyvesant town were not offered to black renters and so, in a sense, it was a "spiritual" slum, a representation of the Jim Crow laws it sought to counter.[34]

Harlem of the early 1960s saw a pall of permanent poverty settle over large parts of it. It was an area of great contradictions. And to many, it was home. Roy Innis remembers this aspect of it:

> "...for the masses of the ghetto dwellers this was a warm and familiar milieu, preferable to the sanitary coldness of the middle-class neighborhoods and a counterpart of the communities of the foreign-born, each of which has its own distinctive subcultural flavor. The arguments in the barbershop, the gossip in the beauty parlors, the "jiving" of bar girls and waitresses, the click of the poolroom balls, the stomping of the feet in the dance halls, the shouting in the churches are all <u>theirs</u>—and the white men who run the pawnshops, supermarts, drug stores, and grocery stores, the policemen on horseback, the teachers in blackboard jungles—all these are aliens, conceptualized collectively as "The Man," intruders on the Black Man's "turf." When an occasional riot breaks out, "The Man" and his property become targets of aggression upon which pent-up frustrations are vented. When someone during the Harlem riots of 1964 begged the street crowds to go home, the cry came back, "Baby, we a<u>re</u> home."[35]

In 1960, there were 199,637 residents in Harlem of whom 97% were black. Nearly a third of these residents were under twenty years of age, two-fifths were under forty-five, and 55% were female.[36] The population density was very high, with nearly 250,000 people living per square mile.[37] Half of the buildings were built before 1900.[38] A little less than half of them were rated "deteriorating" or "dilapidated"— meaning unfit for habitation.[39] The quality of housing was one of the central complaints of Harlem residents. There were unsafe and unsanitary conditions with rats and roaches a constant presence in many buildings. Violations of building codes were common with broken plumbing, heating, and water units. Rooms were crowded and privacy was rare. Such crowding impacted the children's ability to learn because they had no place where they could prepare for school, and there was constant noise. Even these degraded conditions, though, were expensive: Harlem had some of the highest rental rates in the city.[40]

Most Harlemites held menial jobs; high-paying jobs were closed off to them because of race. The median income was $3,480 per family compared to $5,103 for New York City residents. Only 7% of skilled workers in Harlem were employed. Many employers kept their lowest skilled and lowest paying jobs for the black applicants. This trajectory began in school where guidance counsellors discouraged black students from aiming higher than unskilled or service positions.[41] Unemployment varied between 7% among the 20-44 year olds on up to 30% among teenagers; these averages were far higher than in the rest of the city. By the mid-60s about a third of Harlemites were stuck in substandard employment; even with more education, their salary levels were far below those of their white counterparts.[42] Such low wages kept them living in substandard housing.[43]

Almost all businesses in Harlem were small, the majority being food, beverage, and service businesses.[44] Few of these had more than ten employees.[45]

The schools struggled and generally provided substandard education. Though segregation in New York public schools had been illegal since the turn of the century, virtually all the students in Harlem public schools by the 60s were black. Different plans to integrate schools such as the open enrollment and free choice options did little to remedy the situation. The "Princeton Plan"—the idea of pairing of a white and non-white school—seemed impractical in a complex urban environment.[46] Efforts to study and suggest ways of improving public schooling in Harlem were carried out in the 1930s and 1950s to little effect.[47] The conditions in all aspects of public schooling in Harlem were deteriorating—student achievement, the quality of faculty, and the condition of physical plants. In the 6th grade, 80% of students read below grade level. In the 8th grade, over 80% were below grade level in math skills. In the 1960-61 academic year, 10% of high school students in Harlem dropped out. Of those entering high school in 1959, 53% eventually dropped out.[48]

This downward spiraling vortex of poor housing/poor schooling/underemployment, exacerbated other problems. In the late 1950s, drug use in Harlem increased to ten times as high as the rest of the city, and it grew in leaps each year in the 60s.[49] The homicide rate in Harlem was six times the city average; in the neighborhood between Fifth Ave. and Lenox from 126th and 140th streets, the rate was fifteen times higher.[50] Given such conditions, a disease like TB was still present among the residents of Harlem—one fourth of all the cases in the city.[51]

In the early 1960s, a major effort was put forth to try to address these problems on a broad scale: the Harlem Youth Opportunities Unlimited (HARYOU). Guided in great part by the distinguished psychologist Kenneth B. Clark and with substantial funding from the Federal and local governments, the aim was to study poverty and its many effects in Harlem and to come up with a comprehensive program for youth. The key idea was to empower young people, to give them the tools to better their lives, and to avoid the pitfalls of poverty. A two-year study of Harlem residents was undertaken in which educational standards, poverty rates, dropout rates, IQ's, family structures and challenges, drug use, delinquency—among many other indicators — were all compiled and studied. This was an in-depth effort to understand the "problems of the slums",[52] how such ideas as the self-concept of black people as prisoners of the ghetto contributed to these challenges—especially with the existing racist structures and attitudes of the greater society. The young people of Harlem saw that in the world beyond their world, other young people were learning, working, developing but when they looked at their own world they saw only limitations, lives mired in terrible, seemingly intractable conditions. So, these young people lived in an in-between world: they could neither join that other world because of their race, nor did they want to give up and give in to the cycle of poverty and failure that swirled around them.[53]

After the research period, HARYOU produced an extensive report of its findings and went into the implementation stage with funding from the Great Society programs. The successful programs included the summer camps, the large number of youth who found employment and the strengthening of group identity.[54] Like many other efforts of the Great Society period, HARYOU struggled with the sheer complexity of the challenge—the many programs initiated and the coordination of all of these. More time was needed to scale up the efforts because so many people involved. The demands of the times, though, caused the implementation to be rushed and, in the haste, there was much unevenness in the different programs with some never even reaching fruition.[55] But, ultimately, the entire effort, which by the mid-60s involved millions of federal dollars, foundered on the rocks of local politics—the incumbent Congressman sought to wrest control of the program and turn it into a form of patronage for political power instead of an organization for training and empowerment.[56]

Craig Rothman had left home as a teenager and gone from apartment to apartment trying out different ways of life and belief systems and substances. A teacher, John Czerniejewski, befriends him and took a loving concern for his well-being. He tried to convince Craig that he could be a successful student even though he'd had had a pretty bad academic record. Craig tried to convince John that he had a plan and didn't need an education. He didn't need for anything formal. John persisted.

Because the teenager didn't have a phone, John went to where he was staying at the time in midtown and tacked a note on his door. The note invited him to come up and apply for Harlem Prep because he thought he would do well there.

It was in these streets of pain and promise that Rev. Eugene Callender served. He sought to bring the grace of Jesus Christ and the ministry of healing directly to people, even setting up a dais in a Harlem parking lot from which to preach. By the late 1950s, he had established the Addicts Rehabilitation Center to help combat the exploding problem of narcotics addiction in Harlem.

When he joined the venerable Church of the Master in Morningside Heights in 1959, it boasted a solid middle-class black congregation, a Morningside Community Center, two camps in New Hampshire, and a social work program. This was a well-heeled, powerful congregation.

As he moved through the streets, though, he encountered many youths hanging around smoking dope. He and the church began a program for high school dropouts. But the status conscious congregation was not eager to include troubled youth in the main church building itself.

He became involved in the massive youth empowerment program, HARYOU, as the chairman of the Board. One of his main efforts with HARYOU was to stem the dropout rate in Harlem. Since local youth reacted badly to the word "school", the euphemistically-titled "Academies of Transition" were established to help reintegrate students back into school after having been out on the street. These academies focused on students developing a sense of personal responsibility, believing in themselves, valuing hard work, seeing something greater than they themselves, and equally vital, tutoring was provided. An associate pastor at the Church, who was white, made contact with the Young Life mission on the Lower East Side. Volunteers who were white came up to Harlem to serve in these street academies and some of them even moved up there. Corporate funding flowed in to support these educational efforts. Prominent young playground basketball players were recruited into the academies to attract other kids. Unfortunately these excellent efforts ran aground when the most powerful local politician demanded that his personal programs be funded at the same rate as those of HARYOU. The two organizations were fused into one turning them into a tool for political favor.

Back at the Church of the Master, the 1,100 parishioners and over sixty staff members resisted Callender's invitation to poor people whom the congregants considered "ruffians" and, to Callender's dismay, saw as "not our kind". Hundreds of Harlem youth attended the Church's programs on Wednesday nights staffed by volunteers from Young Life. One morning 300 street youth showed up to go to a Young Life weekend retreat. The large group came into the main church building. When they did not remove their hats for church elders, they were chased out.

Callender saw the declining reach of the Church in America as reflected in his experience—he felt the Church of the Master had had little impact on the local community. So he left the ministry to accept the post of executive director of the New York Urban League in April, 1966. He succeeded in increasing the budget from $200,000 to $2 million. He brought the street academy staff with him to the League. These continued to grow and the Young Life volunteers did much of the day-to-day work such as making sure students got out of bed and went to school, and they helped them with challenges outside of the classroom.

The academies were a success. Now, students were ready for higher learning, but there was no college prep school in Central Harlem. Such a school was needed. In keeping with the Urban League's tradition of inter-racial partnership, Callender found partners for this effort in the persons of the white nuns of the Order of Sacred Heart.

2 ~ An Idea Becomes Real

Elizabeth McCormack put on her lace wedding dress at the age of twenty-two. She was giving herself as a bride to Jesus Christ. She would live with complete detachment from the material world, with pure intentions and in total obedience, surrendering herself to God to be used in service to others.

Her head was shorn so that she could wear the full body habit more easily. She had no material possessions. This traditional Roman Catholic ceremony ushered her into a life in the community of the Religious of the Sacred Heart.

Elizabeth McCormack had been shaped by a Catholic world. Raised in Larchmont, NY, she attended Catholic schools and played with Catholic friends. Physically small but imbued with an energetic spirit, she loved to learn and to question. In elementary school she questioned her teacher about hell and wondered if anyone would actually be in it. Her teacher assured her that she could believe in a hell where there were no people.

Her father headed a successful architectural firm that most famously designed the Williamsburg Savings Bank next to the Brooklyn Academy of Music. The affluent McCormack family enjoyed the results of their earned wealth, belonging to an exclusive country club in Mamaroneck, NY, all while teaching their children sound values. When the live-in family cook was found making the "Heil Hitler" salute, she was let go.

Liz's political leaning developed early. She fondly remembered reading *The New York Herald Tribune* to her grandfather whose eyes were clouded over by glaucoma. She announced all the headlines, and he selected which articles and editorials he wanted to hear. The political orientation of the paper turned her towards the Democrats.[57]

On her visits to her paternal grandmother, she remembers having to listen to the hate-filled ranting of Father Charles Coughlin. While she had a memory of the program coming over the airwaves, its message went over her head. Only later would she learn that this leader of the Christian Front, who was an early adopter of radio for mass communication and counted up to thirty million listeners at his show's peak, had been spreading a virulent anti-Semitism until the Church put an end to his broadcasts soon before the onset of World War II.[58]

Though he was a very successful architect, Liz's father had never gone to college. His own father and brother had died when he was young, and necessity had forced him to go to work.

He remained self-conscious about his lack of formal education which he made up for by reading voraciously. He valued education and wanted the best for Liz, so he took her to visit Manhattanville College of the Sacred Heart. When she stepped into the College President's office, she was struck by a quotation on the wall from a Christian philosopher that asserted the importance of rational evidence in harmonizing philosophy with revelation.

At Manhattanville, McCormack was an eager student who soaked in English Literature, philosophy, and Old English, while maintaining a rich social life. Her rational outlook and her appreciation of the exercise of free will and of a person's innate spiritual dignity would help her in the turbulence of the '60s which called for a combination of flexibility and perseverance.

The end of schooling was the time for a Catholic girl to marry and rear children. World War II had broken out, and many young men were headed to the front in Europe so they wanted to marry. McCormack did not find a young man among her peers who really interested her, and neither did her father find any young men suitable to marry his daughter.

Her personal fulfillment at this college developed along with her great respect for the nuns of the Society of the Sacred Heart who taught her, and she seriously contemplated entering the order. Her role model was her teacher of English and history whose presence, sense of fun, and smartness, formed an ideal for her. She now felt called. Though she had never been pious, she knew this was her vocation.

She had to go meet with the Mother Superior who wanted to see if this young woman's decision was real or a temporary enthusiasm. The

Mother Superior suggested she consider delaying so she could go to graduate school at Columbia University. McCormack responded that entering the order was something she "should do" and "do right away". This was her sacred duty. She did not want a back door. She entered the order committed and awake.[59]

☉

In 1971, Cheryl was attending the prestigious Stuyvesant High School in Manhattan. She wasn't bothered that her fellow students were almost all white, but she couldn't stand that all the teachers taught to a test so that students could achieve an unreasonably high level of test scores. Grades below 85 were considered of no value. She was bored out of her mind. Going there felt like a waste of time, and she began to skip school.

One cold Friday morning in February, she did just that and, instead, she tagged along with her best friend Michelle as she went to her school, Harlem Prep. This school was in a converted supermarket, and everyone there was doing college-level work. The students were not allowed to graduate without a GED and a college acceptance letter.

Cheryl wanted to go to Harlem Prep but Michelle told her there was a long waiting list to get in. Michelle went inside, and Cheryl stood out on the street peering in, wishing she could enter as well.

The Spirit moved her. She went inside, spoke with the administrators, took the tests, and sometime later received her acceptance papers. She brought them to her mother who went ballistic. For her mother, the right path went through the white and affluent world.

☉

"Discovering and revealing the Heart of Christ" was the mystical flame that illumined the mission of the Society of the Sacred Heart:

"We are sent by the Church to communicate the love of the Heart of Jesus. In Him all find their true growth as persons and the way towards reconciliation with one   another.

We participate in the mission of the Church through the service of education."[60]

In the early 1800s Madeleine Sophie Barat made it her mission to transform post-Revolutionary France through education and spirituality. She founded an order with a powerful apostolic drive to educate people, though she herself was drawn to the contemplative life. She served as a spiritual guide, a force for education, and a talented administrator who left the legacy of the Society of the Sacred Heart, a religious Order of over 3,500 members. The Church sainted her in 1925.

One of the sisters of that Order, Rose Philippine Duchesne, sailed for the American continent in 1818. Though her desire was to live among the native peoples, she established the first Catholic schools west of the Mississippi River. She eventually was able to live among the Potawatomi Indians but succumbed to the physical rigors of life on the frontier. She died feeling as though her mission had failed, but, in reality, the schools she had opened became part of a significant international educational network. The Church sainted her in 1988.[61]

The Society of the Sacred Heart was a strict, semi-cloistered order but was changed by the tidal wave that went through the Church—the Second Vatican Council (the 21st ecumenical council of the Catholic Church, but the second in Saint Peter's Basilica). This Council updated practices of the Church's organization and worship, engaged modernity in a deeper dialogue, and re-affirmed fundamental Catholic teaching. Among the most visible of its sweeping changes was the use of vernacular language during Mass instead of Latin. These changes affected all branches of the Church including the Society of the Sacred Heart. The order would no longer be semi-cloistered, the title "Mother" became "Sister", and the nuns would be able to go out and live in the community.

Elizabeth McCormack became President of Manhattanville College soon after Vatican II. By the time of her appointment, Liz had earned a PhD from Fordham University in philosophy and had been head of the Sacred Heart School in Greenwich, CT. The College was born in a three-story house of the Lower East Side of Manhattan in 1841 as the Academy of the Sacred Heart, a Catholic boarding school for girls, which had subsequently become a significant educational institution in New York with an emphasis on bettering the world.[62] For decades, students at Manhattanville volunteered in communities in need as an extension of the school's Christian mission which included the breaking down of racial barriers. Harlem was, by these years, in economic and social distress.

In her role as president of the college, McCormack had influence in Harlem and knew many of the prominent people there. Among these Harlemites was Rev. Eugene Callender who expressed his interest in starting a college preparatory high school in Central Harlem—where there was none—to help those who were going through the street academies or had dropped out of the public system altogether. To make this vision a reality, McCormack drew on her able human resources at Manhattanville, especially the talents and energy of Sister Ruth Ann Dowd.

Dowd had joined the college in 1949 and taught philosophy, as well as being an advisor and class warden. After eighteen years in this position, she wanted to become more directly engaged in educating women and minorities. American society was changing, pushed in part by the Civil Rights Movement plus a rising generation of idealistic young people, and Vatican II had opened the way for a Catholicism that could be more directly involved in the issues of society. She was experienced in both education and the inner city. She taught an In-Service Seminar on Compensatory Education to public school teachers in Westchester County, NY, as a member of the Education Department at Manhattanville, and was organizing Project SHARE, a program for high-risk, high-potential students from the urban low-income neighborhoods.[63]

The discipline, training, and expectation of obedience with which the sisters in the Order had been inculcated may well have helped Dowd overcome any hesitation that such a challenge might cause; speaking later:

> "In the old days, as a nun, you did what you were told …, If someone told you that you could climb a flag pole, then maybe you should try."[64]

Dowd was not afraid to turn her commitment to social change on her own college. During that time, she challenged the alumnae:

> "Is every alumna, after reading the Report of the President's Commission on Civil Disorder, asking Manhattanville some hard questions about its student body and its curriculum, its relevance to the era of great cities? Are you aware of how many black students are on campus? Of the attitude of white students towards them? Has Manhattanville any black men on its faculty? Does African

civilization takes its place in the curriculum alongside East Asian Studies? What is Manhattanville doing to prevent our nation from "rapidly moving towards two increasingly separate Americas"? ... are you satisfied that the College is carrying its weight of social responsibility? ... The atmosphere these days is charged with messages. Are we on the right wave length to receive them? ... What about those of us who have so much?" [65]

Such passion and discipline helped her leave the security of her professorship in philosophy for the risk of an inner city start-up school with an ambitious goal:

"In the 1960s there were no college prep schools in Central Harlem. Our goal was to bring in high school dropouts and prepare them for college. We promised that if they were able to complete the program, we would place them in colleges."[66]

This school would be the realization of this aspiration. Later, Dowd reflected on the school's underlying philosophy:

"...the most insignificant possibilities for breakthrough in the inner city focus on the adolescent. Head Start programs, the introduction of new techniques in elementary grades will bear little fruit as long as the teenager and the "just beyond," who stands as models for the growing boys and girls, are themselves alienated members of society. The values of the adolescent are readily by the younger members of the block. An image of black youth must be presented to the ever-increasing numbers of children growing up in the Harlems of today. And to the adolescent must be offered the opportunity for further education and they must be motivated to seek it. The tragedy of the ghetto is the appalling fact of wasted human talent. It is a waste that America can ill afford."[67]

Study Group with Sisters Ryan, Dowd and Early

Ed was raised by a single mother and his grandparents. He lost his only father-figure at age six when his grandfather died which was the defining moment of his life. He was a very shy and sometimes angry boy.

In fifth grade he entered a program for "Intellectually Gifted Children" (IGC) which took him to a school way outside his neighborhood and was his first exposure to white kids. It felt odd and his school career was very shaky. School always bored him, and he was eventually removed for truancy.

He was accepted at the elite Horace Mann Country Day School for Boys for the 9th grade—his older brother had graduated from there—but only lasted one semester. Being with very rich kids was too much for him; one of them said to him, "I've never seen a Negro in person before". He was expelled from his next school and went to work full-time at sixteen.

He managed to get a general diploma and be interviewed by Harvard University but felt uncomfortable about that school. To get his high school diploma he went to 369th

Regiment Armory where the new college preparatory school, Harlem Prep, was welcoming students for its first year.

On June 7, 1967, the New York Urban League, represented by Rev. Eugene Callender, and Manhattanville College, represented by Sister Elizabeth McCormack, signed a joint memorandum stating:

"1) They intend to establish a "modest preparatory school" for boys and girls of the Harlem area who had dropped out of school or are about to drop out,

2) Manhattanville College will provide three persons to serve in this school and one of them shall be the administrator,

3) the New York Urban League "will undertake to obtain the necessary funds for the budgetary needs of the school,

4) the administrator and Board of Trustees shall annually prepare a budget which will be presented to the New York Urban League as a request for the necessary funds,

5) the administrator will use the help of street workers employed by the New York Urban League to recruit properly motivated students, "act as some control upon such students," and secure community acceptance of the program."[68]

The college preparatory school would be the third in a series of steps envisioned by the New York Urban League for its educational program. First, students were recruited off the street into "street academies"—storefront classes designed to encourage them to continue with their education. Second, those who demonstrated the motivation would go to an 'academy of transition' to receive remedial help as needed. And the third and final step would be attendance at this new college preparatory school.[69]

With the country having experienced a great civil rights awakening and the Federal government making the fight against poverty the centerpiece of its domestic policy, this project attracted a group of prominent New Yorkers to serve as its first Trustees. In addition to Callender and McCormack, the initial Board included the Hon. Cyril D.

2 ~ An Idea Becomes Real

Tyson, Harvey M. Spears, Percy Ifill, Charles Silberman, Dr. Samuel Proctor, Dr. Henry H. Callard, and John Mosler.[70]

Cyril Tyson graduated from Columbia University's Teacher's College and helped to structure the ambitious HARYOU-ACT project that had been rolled out in Harlem. Harvey Spears fought in World War II, trained at Harvard Law School, participated actively in the city's Democratic politics and wanted to be more involved in helping to solve society's challenges; Whitney Young had advised him to concentrate on education. Percy Ifill graduated from New York University and became a prize-winning architect whose firm designed the 24-story State Office building on 125th Street Charles Silberman wrote books such as *Crisis in the Classroom: The Remaking of American Education* which drew attention to issues of educational inequalities, race, and crime. Dr. Samuel Proctor was an activist preacher and educator who later went on to head the most influential church in Harlem, the Abyssinian Baptist Church. Dr. Henry H. Callard directed Princeton University's Teacher Information and Placement and was the headmaster of the prestigious Gilman School in Baltimore, Maryland, for twenty years. John Mosler chaired the Board of Directors of the New York Urban League and worked as the CEO of the Mosler Safe Company that made the safe for Fort Knox. The Board selected Sister Ruth Dowd to be its administrator, a key position to moving this project from vision to reality.[71]

The New York Board of Regents approved a three-year provisional charter:

> "To establish, conduct, operate and maintain a non-sectarian, private college preparatory school for boys and girls between the ages of 15 and 21 who have dropped out of school and who, in the opinion of the administration of the school can be motivated to complete a secondary education, to provide such education for such boys and girls and to develop liaison with a number of colleges eager and willing to accept such graduates."[72]

The New York Urban League negotiated on behalf of the school to lease a property on Eighth Ave. and 136th currently occupied by a supermarket, Finast, that intended on closing that location.[73] A temporary space would have to be found for the first year.

The approved budget was about $300,000. Anticipating an enrollment of about sixty students, this meant that the spending per pupil would be $5,000. This compared with $1,074 spent per student in the public system.[74]

Among the earliest funders were the Astor Foundation that invested part of the substantial fortune of the Astors—a family that had been known for its lavish lifestyle and then made a turn towards greater social consciousness—in helping others and into preservation, and the Hayden foundation, that focused on investing in children and youth. Soon the Ford Foundation was taking a lively interest. Founded with seed money from the son of Henry Ford, this Foundation gave grants in support of several broad goals: strengthening democratic values, reducing poverty and injustice, promoting international cooperation, and advancing human achievement. With the involvement of John Mosler and the ongoing help of his wife, Sheila Mosler, the Mosler Foundation became another very important supporter of Harlem Prep during the early years.[75]

Along with a Board, funding, and a physical plant, this project of Harlem Prep needed someone to lead who could inspire teachers and students with a sense of mission and purpose and enthusiasm for serving young people. Such a person was found in Edward F. Carpenter. In the fall of 1967, the time had come to open doors and welcome students to Harlem Prep.

3 ~ "Push Outs," Not "Drop Outs"

Ed Carpenter's broad smile, warm gaze, and friendly outgoing demeanor greeted every student who entered Harlem Prep. Each student knew 'Carp', and he knew each student. He conveyed a sense of compassion and openness and was a parental figure to many.

He was also a pied piper. In assemblies and other meetings, he could articulate a vision of possibilities and fire up others with enough enthusiasm to climb mountains and overcome obstacles. He inspired people to collective action: "…we're going to have to go from the 'ego' to the 'we-go' …."

He was in perpetual motion. A student was asked one day in the halls if he knew where Ed Carpenter was, and the student recommended that the visitor stand still because soon enough, 'Carp' would come rushing by. In an emergency, Carpenter once got to Harlem Prep in fifteen minutes from his home in Teaneck, New Jersey.

There were many battles for him to fight, especially in raising funds to keep the school afloat. He was always out and about, schmoozing with funders. He carried himself with self-confidence and got along with people of diverse backgrounds. A "can-do guy"—his retort was always, "How do we figure this out, how do we do this?"

At the time that Ed Carpenter was offered the position of the head of Harlem Prep by Rev. Callender, in the spring of '67, he was working as a guidance counselor and directing a program at Queens College for preschoolers from low-income neighborhoods. A native New Yorker, he had been reared in a brownstone on 131st Street. He attended Frederick Douglass Junior High School and then Commerce High School where he played varsity basketball. He became a second lieutenant in the Army during World War II, during which he served with pride under Colonel De Maurice Moses of the 369th Regiment for forty-two months in the Pacific. After the war, he earned a degree in psychology and math at Long Island University, a Masters in political psychology, and a certificate in advanced guidance.[76]

Carpenter's view of the world was informed by the teachings of the Baha'i Faith, an emerging world religion dating back to the mid-19th century. His later doctoral dissertation made frequent references to its teachings. The principles in his educational philosophy reflected the universalism found in the Baha'i Faith: the oneness of the human race, the equality of men and women, unity in diversity, the unity and progressive nature of religions, and the inevitability of world peace. Human beings were not simply physical entities moving through the world, they were spiritual beings whose lives had meaning and purpose. Service was an essential component of a student's real education and work done in a spirit of service was akin to worship.[77] He often attributed the success of the school to the Faith's founder. When asked about the reason for the success of Harlem Prep, he often answered "Baha'u'llah", "Baha'u'llah". One reporter misunderstood the foreign-sounding Arabic title and thought that Ed was citing the Swiss philosopher, De Chardin. Ed was clear in his intentions to have a school that reflected Baha'i principles.

Along with Ed Carpenter's charisma, Harlem Prep also greatly benefited from the hiring of his wife, Ann Carpenter. A native New Yorker, Ann had been teaching English at Haaren High School. She brought experience, dedication to young people, and a capacity for organization. Each student found in Ann a warm and caring presence though she did her work with great seriousness. She shouldered many of the tiresome but vital logistics of the day-to-day running of a school—schedules, teacher training/supervision, organization of the curriculum.

Ann and Ed made a formidable team. His fiery inspiration attracted dedicated individuals, and her quiet, no-nonsense organizational skills held it together. The sheer quantity of ideas which would flow through Ed needed shaping to become actualized.

The initial curriculum consisted of English, Mathematics, Biology, American and African History, and current affairs. The focus of the teaching was on the acquisition of skills, self-directed work in which students carried out a self-instructional project, and group inquiry.[78] The original faculty members were the Carpenters, the three sisters from Manhattanville College Ruth—Dowd, Jane Early, and Oonah Ryan—Duane Jones, Dr. Yusef ben Jochannan, Anthony Lewis, and Gaywood McGuire.[79]

Harlem Prep opened officially on October 2, 1967, in the 369th Regiment Armory—the same regiment in which Ed Carpenter had served—on upper Fifth Avenue which had been secured with the help of Harlem physician and civic leader, Arthur C. Logan.[80] Dr. Logan had been the personal physician of Duke Ellington and Billy Strayhorn who composed "Upper Manhattan Medical Group" for him.[81] The 369th was the only all black American regiment in the state. The massive 4,600 square meter brick building gave a foreboding, almost Medieval-like appearance combined with 1930s art deco flourishes.

On opening day, Rev. Callender stood before the students in a borrowed classroom. Behind him was a chalkboard with erased lettering, the faint word, though, was still visible: "hand grenade". He had met with the press prior to this first day and declared: "Anyone familiar with education in the ghetto over the last 20 years sees the need for a revolution in education in this community."[82] To the students, he gave an inspiring vision: "I see before me the future school principals of Harlem. I see the future directors of the Urban League, the future Harlem bankers, businessmen."[83]

Forty-nine students were there on the first day, but that number increased to seventy-one over the course of the year. Three–hundred had applied from the street academies.[84] Twelve already had high-school diplomas, but these were the general ones so they could not be used toward college admission; the other fifty-nine had dropped out of the public system.

In public schools, black students were often subtly discouraged from taking academic courses; courses; during the 1967-8 school year, only 700 of the 30,000 academic diplomas given out in New York City were awarded to black students.[85]

Ed Carpenter referred to "Drop outs" as "Force outs". Student Anthony Hart worried that Harlem Prep had "…the stigma of a dropout school. People think of the dropout as a loser." But in the public system "teachers have no real interest in the students. To them, it's just an eight-hour job."[86] In explaining the commitment of the teacher who wished to teach in Harlem, Ed Carpenter placed his hand over his heart and said, "Teachers have got to have it right here. They've got to become involved in humans; otherwise they'll never reach the black people."[87] According to Carpenter, students need "a teacher who believes in them".[88]

The student body was mostly male. Most students came from Central Harlem and had come from the street academies, though a few came from the lower East Side, South Jamaica, the South Bronx, and Bedford-Stuyvesant in Brooklyn.[89] The school was tuition free; those students who lived near poverty were paid $25 a week provided they maintain an average of 85 or higher.[90]

One of the few female students, Gretchen Knight, had become disillusioned with her public school: "Everything was phony. It was like a prison. In history class, they taught history the way they wanted me to know it. Everything was memorized. There was no discussion. The first day in math class, the teacher gave us a list of things we couldn't do—we couldn't turn a page while she was talking, we couldn't ask questions. She said the front part of the room was her part of the room, and we weren't allowed there because she had 'important things' on her desk." She dropped out seeing no relevance for herself as a young person, but she wanted to make something of her life and "not jump right onto welfare."[91]

Ed Randolph had bounced around from school to school, a bright boy who was easily bored. His upbringing had been unstable. His father had been one of the first black motormen in the city, and even though he didn't live with Ed's mother, Ed saw him around the neighborhood. Ed Carpenter, a family friend, suggested he finish at Harlem Prep so he could go on to college. Determined to make a go of it, he assured a reporter: "We'll surprise this community. We'll show them we can do it."[92]

One of his favorite teachers was Duane Jones, the English teacher who introduced him to Herman Hesse's novel *Siddartha*, a meditative work about a young man's journey of self-discovery, a theme which resonated with the young Ed. Jones also exposed him to new movies. A graduate of the University of Paris, Sorbonne, Jones went on to public acclaim as the first black actor to star in a horror film when he played "Ben" in the hugely popular cult horror film "Night of the Living Dead".

A teacher whose course stunned Harlem Prep students was Yosef ben Jochannan. In his class, students—most for the first time—heard that Egypt, located on the continent of Africa, pre-dated Greco-Roman culture and the world of the Bible. Many black students were shocked to learn of ancient African contributions to civilization and to see "black" people as having more than a history of enslavement. This learning broadened their horizons, aroused their curiosity, and reflected the growing awareness about race and culture that was a part of the new generation. "Dr. Ben" as he was affectionately known to his students, wore the African Nationalist button of Marcus Garvey's Universal Negro Improvement Association on his lapel. His classes assured students that African history was not inferior to European history. He asked his students rhetorically, "What did Europe have over Africa? Gunpowder, not superior intellect!" as he banged his hand on the table. Students came to him believing that the continent of Africa was like the one depicted in Tarzan movies, with people swinging on vines and sometimes eating each other. He explained his goal:

> "I try to stimulate in these youngsters a sense of pride based on theirancestral heritage. The black child needs something more than George Washington, Betsy Ross and all those whites as persons to emulate. Each group, Irish, German, Poles, and blacks need its group heroes. So I tell youngsters about ancient black Egyptians, such as Imhotep, the great physician of the Third Dynasty, who was the father of medicine long before Hippocrates. I tell them of three Africans most instrumental in making Christianity what it is today: Tertullian, Cyprian and Augustine. I tell them of black Roman Emperors such as Septimius Severus and Caracalla."[93]

This course was supplemented by an even greater experience—travel to Africa. Five Harlem Prep students were selected along with twenty others from the area to go on the Urban League's "African Summer Safari Project", to help black students "discover the source of our heritage".[94] Vic Gomez had three goals as a young person: to attend Harlem Prep, to go to Africa, and to attend college. He was never able to realize his ambition to go on to higher education because he died on the trip to Africa. A tree was planted in front of the school in his remembrance and a yearly award given out in his name to honor the determination with which he sought to better his life.

A student for whom such ideas of Africa must have resonated strongly was 20-year-old Melvin Owens who preferred to go by the name "Black Power". Students read Eldridge Cleaver—the self-titled minister of information for the Black Panther party—Malcolm X, and James Baldwin. Young men were searching for new meanings regarding their identity as black people in a powerful white-dominated society. Black Power went with math teacher Gaywood McGuire on a visit to the Horace Mann School in Riverdale, an elite, mostly white school that had backed the Prep's application for a charter. In a logic class there, the teacher asked: "D and B imply P. If D is true and B is false, can D and B truthfully imply P?" Black Power answered: "No. It's all false. Like if you have a house and you say the bedroom is clean, but the living room is dirty. You can't say you have a clean house. You got a dirty house, man." A ripple of appreciative laughter for the clean logic went through the Horace Mann seniors. McGuire felt proud that the Harlem Prep student had stood out in this rarefied academic setting despite the fact that there was no logic class at the Prep.[95]

The enthusiasm in the armory grew over the months as more students came to Harlem Prep despite the challenges of running the school on a shoestring. Everyone pulled together, especially on rough days:

"It rained almost without letup throughout the day, and all the months of planning and fund raising and work that went into starting the Harlem Preparatory School were almost washed away.

Recalling that day in October, 1967, Edward F. Carpenter, himself a product of Harlem, a former teacher and now headmaster of Harlem Prep says:

The ceiling came down and water was everywhere. Kids grabbed mops—they bought the mops and borrowed the pails. Teachers, nuns, everybody helped. We had school. It was damp and miserable but we had school."[96]

The teachers were on a mission. Sister Ryan dressed in complete black habit that included formal headgear and discussed with her small group of students an aspect of the story they were reading in her English class. In the math class, four young men—including "Black Power"—sat in folding chairs listening attentively to Gaywood McGuire explain a point about sets at the chalkboard. "Dr. Ben" in a short sleeved white shirt and black tie passionately asserts a point about African history to the enthusiastic response of his students who wanted to jump out of their seats with excitement. A young woman in a skirt and white shirt copied down in her spiral notebook the lyrics to "Lift every voice and sing", the "African American national anthem" by

James Weldon Johnson and his brother John, in preparation for a program.

Whitney Young, the National Executive Director of the Urban League, the organization that spurred the founding of the school, praised the success of the Harlem Prep effort:

"Last month I visited with the youngsters of Harlem Prep. ...

These youngsters were branded by the system as impossible to educate. The authorities said they couldn't learn; that they weren't college material; that they were unruly.

Well. I've spoken to many student groups around the country, including several in Ivy League colleges. I've talked with students who grew up not in urban ghettos but on fancy estates with servants to trim the lawns and take care of the house while the family vacationed in Europe. But I have never spoken to a more intelligent group of young men than those of Harlem Prep.

They were smart, assured, bright. Their questions were to the point, revealing that they had thought long and hard about who they were, what they wanted, and where the country is going. ...

They know that they grew up with the cards stacked against them but they are determined to deal a new deck for themselves—to go on to college and to help their community....

At Harlem Prep, college is a living reality, not just something for white youngsters. ... Why are these schools (street academies) succeeding while the city system is failing? The basic answer is that the teachers care; they lavish time and attention on these young men and women which they couldn't get in the public schools. They start with the assumption that their students can succeed. They see no reason why three out of four ghetto youngsters shouldn't go on to college, just as they do in the more affluent suburbs."[97]

The school year bore fruition in all of its students being accepted to colleges: the State University of New York, Fordham University, Berkeley, New York University, Wesleyan University, Vassar College, Utica College, Park College ... Sister Dowd was instrumental in helping students with college acceptance including Ed Randolph who would attend the State University of New York at Stony Brook. The first commencement of Harlem Prep took place on June 17th, 1968. The new head of the Board of Trustees, Stephen J. Wright, greeted the graduates; he was an accomplished musician, an experienced educator—both as a teacher and a principal—who would later be president of Fisk University and, later, the United Negro College Fund.[98] The students wore their dark-blue jackets bearing the Harlem Prep emblem of two crossed spears on an African shield and the words "Moja Logo" (Unity and Brotherhood). A formal ceremony ensued in which a student lifted up the American flag while the others rose to recite the Pledge of Allegiance. Whitney Young, head of the Urban League that helped start the school, and actor Ossie Davis, the actor whose career had begun in the '30s in Harlem and had been one of only a handful of black actors to find roles which went beyond stereotypes, addressed the new graduates. Students Debra Morris, Albert Napoleon, and Murray Parsons spoke to their classmates of dedicating their lives to helping others accomplish what they all had that year. As former dropouts, these students could become important motivators of other young people. Sister Ruth Dowd then introduced the class, and Ed Carpenter gave a diploma to each student—to James Davis who was making his way to Wesleyan University, Leroy Robinson who would be attending Fulton-Montgomery Community College ...

The first year of Harlem Prep had succeeded.

Ed Randolph memorialized this passage in his life:

"Ballad of Edmondo Hattemanne

And tomorrow I shall graduate
And mother will be so proud
As I accept my diploma respectfully
And shadows darkly cloud
My dropout soul, my dropout self.
Sold for sheepskin paper
Sold to make mother happy
A truly comic caper

Five years I spent in high school
Learning much more than they could teach

And tomorrow my dropout
Soul must rise above the crowd and preach

Loudly of the futile wars crying to the armies
Preach loudly to the old time folks
Oh how they'll feel so sorry

And their minds yes theirs alone
Will be so restlessly yearning
To find out why on graduation day
I set my diploma burning."

For Americans, 1968 was a turbulent year. The era was climaxing in extreme opposites—great inspiration and deep discouragement, pride and dishonor, dynamic social change and complete retrenchment. The Tet offensive in March shocked the American authorities and public by showing that the Vietnam War was a long way from being won because the Viet Cong were still capable of strong resistance. Americans ate dinner watching television news programs that showed the brutality of this guerrilla war and the suffering of American soldiers and ordinary Vietnamese people. Popular support was eroding rapidly. President Johnson's energy was spent, and he announced in March that he would not run for re-election. The American military had been dishonored in the minds of many young people as news came out of massacres of innocent Vietnamese villagers by American soldiers and that the government had lied about the actual state of the war and the number of casualties. The upliftment provided by a civil rights movement that had been personified in the unifying and inspiring figure of Martin Luther King Jr. turned to deep discouragement with his murder in April 4, 1968, and the subsequent despair was expressed in widespread rioting; in June 5, 1968, Robert Kennedy, an avowed supporter of civil rights, was also killed. The whole movement had bifurcated into King's approach and a much more radical edge. The more traditional approach resulted in the Civil Rights Act of 1968 signed by President Johnson in April which contained the Fair Housing Act making it a federal offense to discriminate in housing on the basis of race. The summer, though, saw open gun fights between much more militant black groups and the police in Cleveland and Oakland. A conservative white backlash was emerging with the nomination of Richard Nixon as the Republican candidate for president.

The '60s also brought self-examination and reform to the behemoth that was the New York City public school system. One reality was verifiably clear: children in low-income districts were not being adequately educated by the public schools, and most of these children were black and Puerto Rican. Solutions were explored such as different schemes for integration, decentralization of the Board of Education, and community control of individual schools. The principal players in this educational drama were the Board of Education, the Teachers' Union (UFT), antipoverty groups, integrationists, militant black leaders and separatists. In broad strokes, the UFT was concerned with the rights of its members and the anti-Semitism of activists, and the activists were concerned about the persistent low performances of the schools. The UFT fundamentally wanted to have much less, if any, parental involvement in schools, while activists wanted the community—an unspecified entity—to run the schools. Both positions would prove to be problematic.

Decentralization and centralization of the main Board of Education were also both problematic choices. A decentralized administrative structure would balkanize the city into small units that would pass below press scrutiny and would be susceptible to corruption. Centralization created a bureaucracy that was enormous and therefore inefficient and inflexible. Such a large organization also would seek to protect the jobs and status of adults rather than respond to the needs of children:

> "The present quagmire of public education is entirely the result of unworkable centralization and the lust for control that permeates every bureaucratic institutions."[99]

The March on Washington had breathed new energy into the integrationist movements. The community organization CORE (Congress for Racial Equality) aimed its strategy directly at the neighborhood schools. The school system in New York City was set-up in such a way that children were expected to attend their neighborhood public school, as it was supported by the taxes of the local residents and was a manageable distance from the students' homes. This zoning, though, was at the heart of why some schools were all-white and some all-black—they reflected the housing patterns which were greatly influenced by racial attitudes. In the 1950s, white neighborhoods had vigorously opposed the forced bussing of black students from other districts.

Some leaders came to see integration as implying that black people could not raise the standards of the schools in their neighborhoods, and that, somehow, bringing in white students would improve them or that it would simply maintain an unequal status quo:

> "Why do Black people seek control over their local schools? After watching the failures of the present school system, they have concluded that those in control of that system define its objectives in terms of white America. The present authorities use such phrases as "the entire system" of "Negroes aren't the only ones who need better schools." Activists, however, recognize these as euphemisms for maintenance of the degrading *status quo*. The tragic fact is that, regardless of intentions, Black Americans are treated not as full participants in the society but essentially as a group to be considered after the interests of others are attended to. So long as this remains true, school programs will continue to draw heavily on white, middle-class assumptions."[100]

Others saw separate schools as a return to a fictitious "separate but equal":

> "In the years 1965 to 1967 another formidable and insidious barrier in the way of the movement towards effective, desegregated public schools has emerged in the form of the black power movement and its demands for racial separatism. Some of the more vocal of the black power advocates who have addressed themselves to the problems of education have explicitly and implicitly argued for Negroes' control of "Negro schools." Some have asserted that there should be separate school districts organized to control the schools in all-Negro residential areas; that there should be Negro Boards of Education, Negro superintendents of schools, Negro faculty, and Negro curricula and materials. These demands are clearly a rejection of the goals of integrated education and a return to the pursuit of the myth of an efficient "separate but equal"—or the pathetic wish for a separate and superior—racially organized system of education. One may view this current trend whereby some Negroes themselves seem to be asking for a racially segregated system of education as a reflection of the frustration

resulting from white resistance to genuine desegregation of the public schools since the *Brown* decision and as a reaction to the reality that the quality of education in the *de facto* segregated Negro schools in the North and the Negro schools in the South has steadily deteriorated under the present system of white control.

In spite of these explanations, the demands for segregated schools can be no more acceptable coming from Negroes than they are coming from white segregationists. There is no reason to believe and certainly there is no evidence to support the contention that all-Negro schools, controlled by Negroes, will be any more efficient in preparing American children to contribute constructively to the realities of the present and future world..."""[101]

Integrationists—some of the most vocal were white (EQUAL)—insisted that the Board of Education produce a timetable for full integration and commit to it, even if this meant involuntary transfers. In 1964, there were two major boycotts demanding integration.

With the passage of major civil rights legislation in the mid-60s, the movement that had done so much to awaken large segments of the American population was waning. Rising expectations brought on by its success could not be met in short order. As a result, anger continued to foment in low-income neighborhoods. The community action approach also foundered because once community organizations were created, there were low participation rates in elections for their boards plus issues of power and patronage at the local level. Meanwhile, the Board of Education seemed ineffective in being able to tackle the city's educational problems, especially in the area of disparity of outcome. A journalist wrote a scathing and widely read critique:

> "No other sizable city in America spends as much as 70 percent of what New York City spends per pupil, and, despite all the propaganda to the contrary, only a few suburbs spend more ... Public confidence in the system is fearfully low and dropping: white children are leaving the city public schools at a rate of "40,000" a year. ... Even worse, the Negro middle class has almost disappeared. Of the Negro leaders of the integration drive...not one has or has had a child in a New York public school ... All change is resisted because it implies a criticism of the present—and feared, because it will be made without consulting the teachers who

will have to live with the results. The hope for leadership has been disappointed so often that people have been turned in upon themselves, learned to live with meaningless and fantastically detailed rule books, lost any sense of the possibilities outside the narrow structure of the hierarchy of jobs."[102]

In 1966, a new school, I.S. 201, was opened in East Harlem. Local leaders pushed for community control and for the school to affirm the strengths of black culture. I.S. 201 rejected integration, the Board of Ed, and its middle-class white values. They thought that a black school could and should be improved. Parents in the district distrusted the Board of Education, so they opposed its appointing an experienced, well-regarded, white, Jewish principal. A struggle for power ensued between the parents/community organizers and the Board of Education. The school only opened after a boycott and under police protection but with no sense of satisfaction.

In a district in Brooklyn, the head of CORE demanded that all principals submit to him their plans for bringing their schools up to grade level. Teachers in the district felt threatened and looked to the UFT for legal protection. The UFT was very vulnerable to criticism in these districts because it was more than 90% white/Jewish, though its head had been born into poverty in a Jewish family and had been raised as an activist with socialist leanings. The UFT wanted more per pupil spending for students with special needs and for the right to suspend unruly students, a position which came to be seen as a racist cover for ridding a classroom of a black child who did not conform. This confrontation in Brooklyn also hinged on the power to hire and fire teachers and administrators.

The criticism by academicians of the public system was intense: the schools repressed children's natural curiosity and love of learning, imposed middle-class white values on black people, and were not involved in social change. A true community school in low-income areas should provide other services beyond simple schooling; it should become:

"1) the facility where the community begins to meet its latent needs for recreation and fun;

2) the place where the community begins to formulate its efforts to express itself through art, music, drama, etc..;

3) the locale for shaping community policy as it relates to housing, traffic, health, education, and other social issues; and

4) the arena for development and implementing mutual-aid programs designed to aid the less   fortunate in dealing with their problems."[103]

The Board was attempting a process of decentralization. It also designated specific districts as educational demonstration projects such those in East Harlem and the Ocean Hill section of Brooklyn. Ocean Hill was a very low-income area with almost no one holding down a white collar job. Narcotics were a plague—Ocean Hill had one of the highest rates of drug use in the country. These projects suffered from a lack of clear guidelines and expectations especially in terms of funding. The lack of responsiveness by the central Board caused parents to continue to see the Board as an adversary:

"At first, the I.S. 201 (East Harlem) activists attempted to elicit the agreement of the New York City Board of Education to conduct an experiment in community control of a school. The responses were evasive, perfunctory, or nonexistent. This is not surprising. As in most U.S. cities, the Board of Education is expected to represent *all* the people, and it has an established and unwritten policy that requires consensus. Yet, in most cases, consensus guarantees that the interests of the ghetto will be overlooked."[104]

In the Spring of 1968, the governing board of the educational demonstration project in Ocean Hill was frustrated by having the Board of Education deny it authority to hire and fire teachers which State law prevented the Board from delegating. Ocean Hill sought outright to remove thirteen teachers from its schools whom it felt were sabotaging the project and hoped to gain power simply by asserting it. This firm stance appealed to a sense of racial self-determination, and the judge's orders reinstating the teachers were rejected. By the fall of 1968, Ocean Hill had hired its own teachers while the UFT threatened a citywide teachers strike if its teachers were not protected in Ocean Hill. The situation deteriorated, more militant members of CORE became involved, and the UFT would not budge, so compromise became impossible. Fifty-four thousand teachers walked out on strike for two days in September, then again from the 12th of September to the 30th. The Mayor, the Board of Education, and the State

Commissioner of Education all opposed the UFT. Fifteen thousand teachers rallied at City Hall. Racial antagonism surfaced. Black and Jewish organizations and leaders became alienated from one another. An agreement was reached, but the Board of Education could not have its decisions implemented in Ocean Hill. More organizations lined up against the UFT, and the Board backtracked on previous agreements with the union which then picketed every school in city—except those in the demonstration districts. The crisis dragged on for weeks, burdening parents. An agreement was reached in November in which the Ocean Hill board was suspended, teachers were reinstated and the district was placed under the control of a State trustee. No one was truly satisfied.

There was no viable alternative to the public system or an alternative within it. A school like Harlem Prep established itself as a possible alternative model.

The great, Russian writer, Leo Tolstoy, returned to his large country estates fired up with enthusiasm for education. He founded thirteen schools for the children of his peasants and wrote an essay, "The School at Yasnaya Polyana", in which he worked out a theory for a new democratic education. Tolstoy's thoughts directly influenced A. S. Neill, a Scottish writer who founded the Summerhill School in England, one of the earliest and most famous "free schools". At Summerhill, children and adults were considered as social equals, with children encouraged to follow their interests and choose their own path. They were part of a community in which they assumed responsibility for themselves and others. Much time was given over to free play during which a child could explore. Learning could happen outside of a structured-lesson classroom.

In terms of educational philosophy, Summerhill was the spiritual parent of Harlem Prep, which itself was a part of the "free school" movement that emerged in the '60s.

In keeping with the spirit of the 1960s, the whole approach to public education was called into question, which itself came to be seen as a stultifying, teacher-centered, factory model of education:

"...for most American children there is essentially one public system in the United States and it is authoritarian and oppressive."[105]

In the public system, the teachers were "...obsessed by 'control,' and beneath the rhetoric of faculty meetings was the clear implication that students were a reckless, unpredictable, immoral, and dangerous enemy."[106]

An authoritarian culture is created when the teacher and the lesson were at the center and the students were mere recipients:

"...When a teacher conceives of his task as mere instruction, the accomplishment of a lesson, and when he addresses himself to his pupils as to containers of various capacities into which the information must be poured, he is creating conditions which are fatal to growth. Testing, grading, seating arrangements according to the teacher's convenience, predigested textbooks, public address systems, guarded corridors and closed rooms, attendance records, punishments, truant officers—all this belongs to an environment of control and coercion."[107]

"Free school" thinking encouraged the teacher to give up power, to learn to listen, to be open and available to a child's thoughts, and to allow the needs and interests of the student to lead the teacher's planning.[108] How a teacher thought of students affected how the students performed:

"Teachers' expectations tend to become self-fulfilling, "bad" classes tend to act badly, and "gifted" classes tend to respond to the special consideration that they expect to be given to them if they perform in a "superior" way"[109]

In the open environment of the free school "...a pupil functions according to his sense of himself rather than what he is expected to be. It is not that the teacher should expect the same of all his pupils. On the contrary, the teacher must learn to perceive differences..."[110]

The class becomes a student driven, democratic community:

"A teacher has to learn to go with the class, to respond to their desire to learn about things and not cut off their enthusiasm in the service of getting through the curriculum. It is necessary to take time to solve problems communally. The democratic development of routines and rules and restrictions is as crucial to the development of freedom in an open classroom as the arbitrary imposition of them is central to control in an authoritarian class."[111]

The First Street free school did away with all the traditional structures of control found in traditional schools:

"We made much of freedom of choice and freedom of movement, and of reality of encounter between teachers and students; and of the continuum of persons, by which we understood that parents, teachers, friends, and neighbors, the life of the streets, all form one substance in the experience of the child. We abolished tests and grades and Lesson Plans. We abolished Superiors, too—all that petty and disgusting pecking order of the school bureaucracy which contributes nothing to the wisdom of the teachers and still less to the growth of the child. We abolished homework (unless asked for); we abolished the category of truant. We abolished, in short, all of the things which constitute merely an external order; and, in doing this, we laid bare the deeper motivations and powers which contribute to what might be called 'internal order' i.e. a structure of activities based on the child's innate desire to learn, and ... the needs of children the natural authority of adults, the power of moral suasion..., and the deep attachment and interest which adults inevitably feel toward the lives of children."[112]

The free school movement raised the call for a more child-centered approach to education. A. S. Neill's thought influenced a new generation of educational reformers such as Paul Goodman, Edgar Z. Friedenberg, Herb Kohl, and Jonathan Kozol, among many others. And it was the underlying philosophy of Harlem Prep, soon to be one of the most successful of the early free schools.

4 ~ Student-Centered Versatility

"There is a thin line between making it in the ghetto and being busted. Success is a journey and not a destination: a place to go rather than a place to have been. It is a trip through the maze of tenement streets that lead to a deadend, or out. Unfortunately, success and education have not always been seen as synonymous in the ghetto. Indeed, for many black youths, if education has any synonyms, they are pain, rejection, frustration, misunderstanding, alienation, and failure. Harlem Prep offers a new concept of success in education. Success is no longer what you are or where you came from. Success is what you are becoming. Harlem Prep opened on October 2, 1967, as a privately financed, independent preparatory school. Among the students enrolled are the drop-outs and the under educated, those who managed to finish high school but found they didn't have a proper diploma or that they hadn't taken the right courses to go to college. It is not a simple aspiration: to want to go to college.   Harlem Prep has no home. Presently, Harlem Prep is located in two rooms and the corridors of a state armory. Dim lighting, poor acoustics, and cramped classroom quarters make the armory inadequate as a school, especially for a school like Harlem Prep."[113]   (Harlem Prep promotional material)

On August 24th, The New York chapter of the Urban League, acting as the agent for the Harlem Prep school, contracted to purchase a building that had been used as a supermarket at 2535 Eighth Avenue. Thanks to a $100,000 grant from the Mosler Foundation, the renovation was carried out over the summer of '68 so that Harlem Prep could move into their new home in the fall. The plans were for the school to grow to 120-150 students.[114] The title was transferred to the Harlem Prep school on May 10, 1968, and the building was renovated by the architectural firm of Haase and Jackson who wrote the above funding plea.

The interior of the old supermarket developed quickly. James Rogers, class of '69, remembers the changes:

"It's not the same place for more than a week. When we first came to the building, there were no blackboards, or study tables, or even, to some extent, books. The school was one spacious room, contrasting drastically to the large, many-cubicled standard secondary school buildings. You can imagine it: a supermarket, minus the shelves and counters. But that was the first week. For a while, book-shelf partitions were erected between classroom areas, where once, only space made one class distinct from another. Now the library is shelved on lower book cases, and once again, there are no physical dividers between classes. The atmosphere of the building has been softened by a new acoustical ceiling and a black-flecked green carpet covering the entire school floor."[115]

One entered the school through a door on the left and passed the reception desk and offices into a large open area. Sun light poured in through a huge skylight relieving the monotony of an enormous, flat ceiling and brightening the former semi-darkness. The depersonalized supermarket had been changed into an exciting learning space.

Chairs, tables, and low movable partitions designed by Herman Miller, a major manufacturer of modernist furniture credited with inventing the office cubicle, allowed the space to be changed according to the needs of the school program.

Carpeted floors reduced the transmission of sound, enabling concentration. This gave more of a feeling of home than one would get in the cold and indifferent interior of the average public school.

One walked down a large open stair in the main floor to enter the cafeteria and lounge area in the basement. For quiet study, one went up to the mezzanine where there were cubby-holes. Here, one could have a change of pace and disengage from all the activity on the lower level while still being able to lean over and observe the students below.

Arranging Floor Space

Learning, resting, engaging, disengaging, reading, eating, all happened in this open educational ecosystem. No aspect of schooling was compartmentalized. This culture of participation increased a student's curiosity and willingness to take risks for learning.[116]

The organization of the curriculum reflected this flexible, open approach. There were core courses along with courses that focused on particular interests to the student body such as African History. The faculty would gather, sit in a circle—some smoking— and engage in lively consultations on what they'd like to teach in the coming year. Once a set of offerings had been finalized, the course descriptions were typed up, and the students would then choose seven of eight classes from these. The schedule was modular and flexible with classes varying in length from half an hour to two hours. All of this helped to create a learning environment which would allow for the greatest student interest and, therefore, investment. Ann Carpenter then patiently and laboriously put the course selections together and created a schedule. Her consistency and exactness in this task allowed the school to maintain its flexibility.

Hussein with Robert Wilkin, Harlem Prep teacher

"The road that has the bumps and the rocks and the trees with the thorns must have the ripest fruit and that's the road I must take." John Collins, Harlem Prep student

Hussein Ahdieh's father finished writing down by hand the last words of his memoirs on the night before died. He had sacrificed much for his family members. Many of them had emigrated to the United States to flee the religious persecution against the Baha'is in the small town of Nayriz in southern Iran. His son, Hussein Ahdieh, had become the assistant principal of the Harlem Prep school in this very foreign country.

Hussein Ahdieh barely made it out of early childhood having suffered a serious accident, the constant public bullying by local Muslim children whose parents had been egged on by fanatical clerics, and even abduction by a stray dog that had picked up the blanket in which he was wrapped and sleeping. He had lost family members to the senseless religious violence that local Muslims carried out against their Baha'i neighbors, and never doubted that their prayers had protected him in his emigration.

He and his family left Nayriz on top of a truck full of almonds, walnuts , and figs. He was six years old.

He knew nothing of the United States except what he had seen in Westerns and Laurel and Hardy movies. He applied to the famous universities of Columbia and Harvard. His whole family came to see him off when he got his visa.

After stepping off the boat from London, he came to discover that he had not applied nor been admitted to "Harvard" but to "Howard" University which—in a Persian accent—sounds identical to "Harvard". Since the educational and other life plans of immigrants were driven entirely by necessity which, for a young Iranian, meant becoming a doctor or an engineer. He could not do medicine and so chose engineering but Howard did not have such a program.

He went to Saint Michaels College in Vermont in April of 1961. The college cafeteria was full of foods like milk and chicken which were highly prized in Nayriz yet, here, they were in abundance. Seeing that there was a milk machine that would dispense limitless quantities of milk with the lowering of a handle, he drank a lot of milk. Wondering where this bounty came from, he walked out back to look for the cows.

Unable to afford the tuition of this bountiful college, he left for New York City where he rented a room at 76th and Broadway for $7 a week in a building full of drifters and social undesirables among whom he made friends. Once when had the flu he experienced a rare instance of kindness when the woman next door made chicken soup for him. One night, though, after he had not been able to pay the rent, he found his lock jammed and had to spend the night on a bench on Broadway.

He worked wherever he could—a paintbrush factory, a garage, a hotel for prostitutes, the Belford Hotel. He settled into washing dishes in the back of restaurants for several years. At least this way he was fed and made some money. He paid a dollar to an agency called Roma that found him a job each night. He never knew where or when he would work, but the restaurants constantly needed cheap labor. One night he was working in an Italian restaurant in Brooklyn during a big wedding.

He washed hundreds of dishes; dirty and sweaty, he took a break and went out back. He could hear music and, through the window, watched people doing the Twist. Someone complained about his appearance, and a manager physically threw him out through the revolving door. He hit his head and, bleeding profusely, and was taken to an emergency room. When he got out, he returned to the restaurant for his wages, the manager chased him out of his office while cursing at him.

Hussein was stressed emotionally, broke, and couldn't quite figure out how to fit into this new environment. Frightened of being deported, he had to enroll in a school to keep his visa—he was frightened of being deported—, but he also had to work to pay for his tuition. He began to attend Fairleigh-Dickinson University in New Jersey and paid a $100 for a Chrysler which broke down frequently. He got a speeding ticket and had to appear before a judge who asked him why he hadn't paid his ticket. Hussein addressed him as "Your highness" to which the judge replied, "Your honor will do", and explained to the judge that he had been on his way to a school exam. The judge concluded, "Oh, I see 2you've chosen the lesser of two evils—court or an exam" and suspended his license for sixty days. He pleaded with the judge that this would impact him terribly. The next day Ahdieh's photo was on the front page of the local newspaper accompanied by the headline "Hussein Ahdieh from Israel has made a bad choice."

His education in Iran had prepared him well for university, and he made the Dean's list at Fairleigh-Dickinson. Despite the constant fatigue and financial pressures weighing him down, he managed to finish degrees in engineering and European Intellectual History.

Back in Iran, the only thing he had ever known about African people was that the head of the Baha'i Faith, Shoghi Effendi, had greatly praised African Baha'is and loved them very much. It was while toiling in the restaurant kitchens, he got to know black Americans for the first time. He saw the white racism towards his fellow workers and realized that they were the "underdogs" in American society, a status with which he identified as an immigrant. He had also been a part of the persecuted Baha'i minority in Iran. In college his friends were very involved in civil rights and dreamed of having the same thing happen in Iran. A group of his Baha'i friends consulted on starting a school as a way to better society. His first real experience with the civil rights movement was driving with a car full of friends to the March on

Washington where they spent the night in the car because they could not afford a hotel room. His more radical Persian friends identified with the civil rights cause in the U.S. because they wanted justice in Iran against the tyranny of the Shah and so identified with the civil rights cause in the United States.

Gradually, Ahdieh's life improved. He married Tahirih, a medical student from Iran; the young couple scrimped by with a forty dollar turkey-and-cookie wedding in a friend's apartment. Two children were born to them, and they became involved in the work of the local Baha'i community—raising funds, buying a Baha'i center, organizing meetings, teaching classes, and giving hospitality to well-known Baha'i travelers from abroad.

With a full academic load, community service responsibilities, and a young family to support in a one bedroom apartment in Queens, Ahdieh stepped into Harlem Prep. He approached education from a practical perspective, never having had the luxury to reflect on or develop a particular educational philosophy. His views, though, were thoroughly informed by the Baha'i teachings. According to Baha'u'llah, the prophet-founder of the Baha'i Faith, man has a spiritual reality and contained within him are latent capacities that education alone can realize:

"Man is the supreme Talisman. Lack of a proper education hath, however, deprived him of that which he doth inherently possess. Through a word proceeding out of the mouth of God he was called into being; by one word more he was guided to recognize the Source of his education; by yet another word his station and destiny were safeguarded. The Great Being saith: Regard man as a mine rich in gems of inestimable value. Education can, alone, cause it to reveal its treasures, and enable mankind to benefit therefrom."[117]

He admired the work of other Baha'i educators such as Dr. Daniel Jordan and Dr. Stanwood Cobb. Jordan developed the innovative ANISA model of education, a holistic approach that sought to transmit knowledge to young people in a cohesive, forward looking framework grounded in reality and experience:

"Anisa, an Arabic word that means the tree of life, symbolically represents never-ending growth and fruition in the context of protection and shelter, and signifies the blending of the usable and fruitful past with a sense of the future… The unifying force of the Anisa theory derives in part from the fact that it extracts and preserves from the past those elements of experience which serve to keep us in touch with reality while creating an awareness of potentialities for development in the future. In other words, it blends knowledge of the past with a vision for the future. To disregard the past would render us impotent to determine where we are going… This pattern of living is devoid of a sense of the future… When educators follow this same pattern professionally, they produce a flurry of hastily conceived and crisis-oriented innovations accompanied by an exaggerated emphasis on change for change's sake."[118]

Cobb founded the Chevy Chase Country Day School and was president of the Progressive Education Association which emphasized experiential learning, critical thinking, collaboration, social responsibility and a more personalized form of education. After a spiritual search, he became a devout Baha'i. He met Abdu'l-Baha, the son of the founder of the Baha'i Faith, five times, and was a founding member of the first Baha'i Assembly of Washington DC. 'Abdu'l-Baha influenced Cobb to consider the importance of the spiritual dimension of education:

"Stanwood Cobb recorded that 'the most important interview' he had with the Master while he was in Paris in 1913. He wrote, 'I was one of the staff of Porter Sargent's Travel School for Boys. On my first visit He inquired about the school and asked me what I taught. I told Him that I taught English, Latin, Algebra and Geometry. He gazed intently at me with His luminous eyes and said, "Do you teach the spiritual things?" 'This question embarrassed me. I did not know how to explain to 'Abdu'l-Bahá that the necessity of preparing the boys for college-entrance exams dominated the nature of the curriculum.
So I simply answered: "No, there is not time for that."
"Abdu'l-Bahá made no comment on this answer. But He did not need to. Out of my own mouth I had condemned myself and modern education. No time for spiritual things! That, of course, is just what is wrong with our modern materialistic "civilization". It has no time to give for spiritual things. 'But 'Abdu'l-Bahá's

question and His silent response indicated that from His viewpoint spiritual things should come first.'"[119]

Ahdieh's spiritual beliefs were integral to his work at the Prep. He was committed to the school's mission and respected the people who ran it. Though he started there as a math teacher, he was soon made the assistant principal primarily responsible for logistics—funding, managing the facilities, organizing the visits of the numerous guests who wished to see Harlem Prep first hand, and putting out the numerous fires and emergencies that arose in the daily life of the school, much less a start-up school in a neighborhood challenged by economic and social problems. One day a math teacher came to tell him that there was a gunman in the school. He found the gunman pacing around upstairs, angry at a student who owed him twenty dollars. Ahdieh calmly suggested that the young man wait outside until after school. Responding to Ahdieh's friendly demeanor, the young man blurted out, "You're no director," and the ice was broken between the two. Eventually Ahdieh gave him twenty dollars out of his pocket to diffuse the situation completely. Later, this same young man came to the Prep as a student.

He and the Carpenters forged an excellent working relationship. Ahdieh admired their dedication and enthusiasm. Aware that the school was very oriented towards black Americans and sensitive to the reality of racism, he preferred to work in the background.

E. Salmon McFarlane worked with Hussein on the day to day challenges of running the school. He had grown up in that area of Central Harlem. He knew the neighborhood and was well-liked by its residents. During World War II, he had served the country with distinction as a black officer, even being held for a while as a prisoner of war—possibly after the Battle of the Bulge—which had been a very rough experience. His family members were longtime residents of Harlem. His grandfather had been in the numbers racket and, at eight years old or so, "Mac" and his brother were sent to live in a rural country upstate to get away from an outbreak of gang warfare. Mac knew the seamier side of society. This proved useful when trouble visited the school, as it frequently did. When disruptive people showed up, he knew just how to handle the situation. He was also a popular teacher of psychology, and like many of the other Harlem Prep teachers, he sought to challenge the conventional thinking of his students.

Henry Pruitt also assisted Ed Carpenter in the day to day management of the school. He had come to the Prep from a Junior High School in the Bronx and, by comparison, he was especially struck by the peaceful atmosphere in the school. All the rival groups from society at large were represented in the student body, but there were no real antagonisms. The inspirational year he spent at the Prep would continue to inspire him as he pursued his doctorate at Columbia and during his fruitful life of public service in education as a principal and, then, head of the Teaneck Board of Ed, among many other positions. Harlem Prep had been an oasis for him. All the students seemed united under the logo in large letters on the walls of the Prep that proclaimed: "Moja Logo" (unity and brotherhood).

"I was wounded in Vietnam and spent a lot of time in the hospital. I suffered a lot of pain and felt that I owe myself something after surviving, and that is to go to college and make something out of myself." Joseph Rhames, Harlem Prep student

George "Sandy" Campbell was searching for his life's path in the late '60s. He was interested in subjects such as Anthropology at Long Island University and Fordham University. He was also drawn to embracing the contemplative life in the Fransiscan Order. His father warned him that he was floundering and needed to find a direction. He questioned, though, the inconsistencies in the Christian faith and decided against entering the order. His father warned him that he was floundering and needed to find a direction.

He came to be interviewed at Harlem Prep by Ed and Ann Carpenter, Anthony Lewis, Mother Dowd, and Elizabeth McLoughlin. He was hired. This was a life-changing event. Soon after beginning in the fall of 1969 the first of his six years in the English Department, he was introduced to a new religion that answered his spiritual questions—the Baha'i Faith, the religion of the Carpenters, Hussein Ahdieh and a few other teachers. The Baha'i Faith had developed from the teachings and life of Baha'u'llah, a prophetic figure from Persia, who taught that a new Divine spiritual day was at hand, that God was speaking again. Baha'u'llah promised that in the coming time, there would be a great ingathering of all the peoples of the world. The oneness of humanity would be firmly established based on important social teachings—the elimination of prejudice and the extremes of wealth and poverty, the equality of the sexes, and the harmony of science and religion, among others.

He found that everything at Harlem Prep reinforced the oneness of humanity. Here was a group of people from a variety of backgrounds dedicated to serving young people, a family trying to create a dynamic learning environment:

"Everything was intricately woven together as a whole. We all came there, initially, from diverse backgrounds for different reasons. Some came as students, some as teachers, some as administrators only to become unified around the same purpose—to become a community of learners and change agents in an environment that could no meet the demands of our awakening spirits.

We started out with different visions of humanity and reactionary attitudes of how to respond to what was present in our society: our dysfunctional homes, our inequitable learning environments, the abrasive living on the streets of our city, the racist and divisive politics of our country and the persistent inhumane treatment of people throughout the world. Out of this negativity, came a family who understood that what burdened my brother burdened me. Most of us came away wanting to make change that would ultimately impact on the potential growth of our own lives and successive generations. We were one!"[120]

Although he was a teacher, he was only a few years older than most of the students and developed sincere friendships with them. They came from all walks of life—different ethnic, religious, and socio-economic backgrounds. His life now had direction and purpose. He had found an arena in which he could exercise his talents and be accepted as an equal. He was part of a family that was helping his courage and confidence to grow.

He found that the poor literacy strategies that the public schools had taught the students had brought them up to little more than an elementary school reading level. But now, these young people found themselves in high school without this important skill. Sandy was determined to help find an answer and guide these students to success.[121]

For Cliff Jacobs, Sandy's class "Being and non-Being" in which Sartre, Kierkergaard, Buber, and Camus, were read, was life-changing. Such reading would never have been permitted in his previous school—a traditional Catholic school that would not have been open to exposing students to the challenging ideas of existentialism. The new ideas broadened Cliff's horizons and engaged his sense of curiosity.[122]

Teaching at Harlem Prep was spontaneous and organized around the needs and interests of the students. Textbooks did not allow for this level of flexibility so teachers often made their own materials. Students and teachers were in a constant dialogue about learning in which students were asked about their interests and teachers allowed their answers to shape the courses.

A strong "esprit de corps" animated the entire Harlem Prep community. There was a shared sense of commitment, a vision of service. In these first years, an evening education program was attempted on Monday through Thursdays from 7 to 10 pm, requiring an extraordinary degree of sacrifice by teachers and coordination between administrators, parents, and teachers. The school was willing to try to go all the way in helping young people:

> "Harlem Prep is a challenge, a pioneer, and a godsend. A challenge to the establishment which has discarded those who wish to be educated and economically better off. A pioneer in rendering educational assistance to these people. A godsend because we all ask where would we be without Harlem Prep?
>
> If Harlem Prep doesn't do anything else for me, or even if I don't make it to college, Harlem Prep has given me self-confidence. A man won't take the first step if he knows he is going to fail."[123]
> (James Rogers, Harlem Prep student, '69)

In addition to the basic curriculum, teachers developed a very popular film department complete with a set on which students could practice and develop production skills. A dynamic group of "Moja Logo" singers, dancers, and drummers, performed at public events in the community. A basketball team excelled as a member of the A.A.U.

The sisters from Manhattanville College served the students of Harlem Prep selflessly and played a vital role in helping to make the school a reality. As a result of Vatican II, they did not live hidden away in a convent but, rather, Sisters Dowd, McLoughlin, and Early, shared an apartment in the neighborhood—a huge change for them from the safe predictability of cloistered living. They also went from wearing full habits to civilian clothes. Together, the three sisters drove their Dodge Dart to school each morning. Fired by the social mission of the Gospels, they were totally dedicated to their service. When other employees arrived early at 7:30, the sisters were already there and when the last employee left at 4:30, they stayed to work. They often offered their pay back to the school; once one of the sisters threw the money up in the air and said, "Jesus keep what you want in the air and let the rest fall to the ground".

Sister Early's care and attention were vital to the success of Lorelei Fields. She had come to Harlem Prep from the street academies after having dropped out of Charles Evans Hughes High School because of pregnancy. With no particular ambitions, she went to the Prep to please her mom. She had little academic self-esteem, but Sister Early was able to reach her. Mathematics had always seemed impenetrably difficult to Lorelei, but Early's patient and enthusiastic instruction helped her have a breakthrough. She even spent some of her lunch hours going over math problems with her teacher. Harlem Prep's large open area with classes all happening simultaneously and the care shown by the teachers gave her the feeling of being in one big family that could raise her up. College, though, did not exist in her world. No one in her family had been to one. Sister Dowd approached her one day as she sat on the couch near the entrance way of the school and brought her into the office to encourage her to visit Marymount College. Though Lorelei did not want to attend a school that had no male students, the seed had been planted. After going to a college fair, she applied and was accepted at Fordham.

Sister Dowd's efforts were crucial to the school's establishment. She worked with the Board of Regents, Ed Carpenter, and Manhattanville College, in getting the school accredited. She was an able and tough administrator. *The New York Times* selected her as one of their women of the year. She was guided by a deep social conscience and was well-aware of the educational foment and the many needs in Harlem.

Sister Liz McLoughlin joined the Harlem Prep staff in its second year, taking the place of Sister Onna Ryan. From a large Irish Catholic family, Liz went straight into the convent. She had loved her teachers at the Sacred Heart High School on Manhattan's Upper East Side, and she, like her mother, had graduated from Manhattanville College; her grandmother had attended a Sacred Heart College as well. She had considered the Peace Corps, because she was curious about foreign countries, but the Corps was not a lifelong commitment. Like Sister Dowd, Sister McLoughlin was passionate about social justice. She wanted to be actively involved in the betterment of society. Prior to Harlem Prep, she had been involved in violence prevention. Though she had not had the opportunity for much interaction with black Americans, she loved all of her students, irrespective of race. The late '60s were heady, turbulent times, and Sister McLoughlin loved being on the cutting edge of her times.

The students did not understand the internal realities of these religious women whom they tended to see as inter-changeable. Sister Liz once met with the mother of one of her Harlem Prep students and anticipated discussing the student. Instead of discussing students, anticipating a discussion about the student. The mother, though, wanted to talk about her marriage, even though Sister Liz was single and only twenty-seven. Another student, a young man, wondered why Sister Liz was depriving the future of her genes by being a nun. Though the Sisters were aware that the students and staff at Harlem Prep may not have understood their committed way of life, this did not deter them from giving themselves over completely to their educational mission.[124]

Sister Elizabeth McLoughlin teaching a course at Harlem Prep

Martha Manley, math teacher

John Czerniejewski was another teacher whose spiritual commitment caused him to be totally dedicated to his students with whom he found both great challenges and great rewards. He had graduated from the University of Hawaii in 1968 with a degree in Marine Biology and moved to the East coast. Soon thereafter he was teaching science at Harlem Prep and living up in the Bronx. He had come from a Polish family and was a stranger to Harlem. Though these were times of high racial tensions, he was willing to cross these barriers and follow his convictions. Once, during a stick-up in Harlem, he confronted the young man wielding a weapon, acted like he believed he belonged there, walked around them and simply continued on his way.

Physically large and emotionally sincere, Czerniejewski was a "gentle giant" given to hearty, infectious laughter; he knew a thousand jokes, humorous stories about growing up with four brothers, and did a spot-on imitation of Curly from the Three Stooges. His ability to see humor in a variety of situations made him an especially memorable teacher. He derived genuine enjoyment from designing science experiments for his classes and spoke with enthusiasm about watching his students grow intellectually and become college-ready.

He greatly admired the Carpenters and shared their Baha'i beliefs. He came from one of the only Baha'i families of Polish Catholic background. The Faith entered this family when he had been struck by a train at two-years old and thrown more than twenty feet. This traumatic event caused his mother to reconnect with God, and she became a Baha'i three years later along with her husband and five sons. An active member of the New York City Baha'i community during his Harlem Prep years, John grew in his convictions and in his sense of service.[125]

John Czerniejewski teaching a course at Harlem Prep

Father O'Brien teaching a course at Harlem Prep

"MOJA and LOGO are written on the wall at Harlem Prep. These two words of African origin for unity and brotherhood have as many meanings as our school's students have diverse experiences. But each one of our lives is united for one immediate aim—to go on to college. As a family helps its members get a start in life, we students help each other toward our common goal.

Harlem Prep really is a family—and not one just in name. People at the school I formerly attended spoke of being a family, but what was projected was the coldness of an institution that paralyzed creative thinking. The difference between that school and Harlem Prep is the difference between my turning out to be a graduate statistic or a creative thinker in whatever field I might choose.

The fact that everyone knows everyone else adds to Harlem Prep's personal character. Even the person with the contrasting point of view is my friend—better yet, my brother. Brotherhood—it's written on the wall, and it's practiced by students and teachers alike. And when you have a school where teachers and students work together, you have a family." (James Rogers, Harlem Prep '69)

In the summer of '69 the staff deepened its commitment to the community by running a large summer program with the help of funding from IBM. Stores in the neighborhood got into the spirit of the program and deeply discounted many necessary items.

Ed Carpenter and Sister Dowd enrolled 500 students for an eight-week program. The target group was 8-14 year olds who were in the streets of Harlem during the summer and according to Ed Carpenter, "subject to the pathologies of the community":

"In addition to wanting to do something for the youngsters, we wanted students who have been in Harlem Prep and went to college, and some of those who just graduated, to work with us.

What is the rationale? To work with the pre-teenagers and teenagers. The reasoning is simple. I think we should a get a quick return on the dollar. If the youngster's been in school for 10 months, he's learned something. We may not be able to measure it, but he can share that with the younger person. And this way we're getting knowledge as quickly as possible back to the community.

But more important: All our students are some sort of leaders of some sort of organizations. I thought it would be a beautiful thing for their groups to observe them with their Harvard sweaters,

Hampton sweaters, Yale sweaters—with the Harlem Prep insignia in their backs—in the community serving. It shows the community that the children are not flying away with a middle-class syndrome to the suburbs."[126]

Attendance at the program went as high as 500 students but other days there were many fewer. No student was forced to attend. They included a Vietnam veteran who had returned from the war after being wounded three times. He heard of the Prep in a pool hall and enrolled because he "...needed more education just to talk to the people I see every day and to cope with the problems around me."[127]

The program ran five days a week from 10 a.m. to 5 p.m.; when the day was over, counsellors preferred to keep the students indoors while they waited for their parents rather than allowing them to hang out in the street. Many students arrived as early as eight a.m. A regular day consisted of learning mathematics, reading, arts, African studies, mental health, hygiene, physical education, and field trips. The mornings were spent in the classroom, while the afternoons were more physically active with athletics, sewing, and interpretive dance. The last period was dedication to relaxation during which students could deepen friendships and unwind.

Much effort was made to stimulate in students a love of learning and to motivate them to stay in school. This required that the students be shown love and concern and be educated from the inside out. The hope was to be able to extend the summer program throughout the year in the form of remediation programs. Ed Carpenter—who was personally recognized in the fall by the *Amsterdam News* as the "Unsung Hero" of October, 1969[128]—stated the ambitious goal of the faculty:

"The young children are the ones who will bring about understanding and peace. And education and training are the keys to improvement. The first time a kid comes in the door at Harlem Prep he knows it's open, it will always be open, there will be honesty and there will be interchange. And we will be servants to them even when they're in school."[129]

"Janet McDonald came out of her apartment on that summer day filled with energy, walked gingerly up the hill, past the expressway, into the High Street subway

station. She had not been able to scrounge up the coins for the "A" train so she leapt over the turnstile, determined to make it down to Harlem Prep.

After drifting through an indifferent public school system that had graduated her, all she could see was possible employment with the phone company. She had bigger dreams and had demonstrated real potential but, also, had grown up in an environment with few role models whose examples she could emulate. Her neighborhood was mired in a poverty that was—to all live-minded young people— an arid desert, devoid of opportunity, encouragement, possibility...

So, after graduating, she found herself sitting in her room depressed and lethargic from her lack of prospects. Then, an ad caught her eye: "You pass the test, we'll do the rest", for the Harlem Prep school. Here was a school that would work to guarantee admission to a good college if a student was willing and able. She suddenly had a new vision of herself as a college graduate involved in something greater than the parochialism of a poor neighborhood in Brooklyn, which she eventually would in becoming a successful author of books for young adults and moving to France.

So that day, she got up, ran out of the door, and took her leap of faith."[30]

In Harlem Prep, Alberto Cappas found a place that could give him the encouragement and opportunity to go beyond the circumstances of his childhood. Born in Puerto Rico, his parents settled in a black and Latino neighborhood at 108th Street and Columbus Ave. His mother reared them well, but no one in his family had ever been to college, so they did not see the value of higher education. He was able to make it through Brandeis High School but only received a general diploma which did not make him eligible for college, and, anyway, his academic performance had not been strong enough. Still, he knew he wanted more out of life. At this point, he heard about Harlem Prep. Five of the young men from his neighborhood ended up there; he was the only Latino.

Harlem Prep was a whole new world. Gangs infested his neighborhood, and young people were filled with negative feelings. But at the Prep, the teachers energized him and his friends with their positive support, nurturing them as though these young men were their own babies being born. Ed Carpenter took the time to get to know each one of them, something which Alberto had not experienced before, and Sister Dowd was very compassionate in understanding their situations.

Harlem Prep's individualistic and supportive philosophy helped Alberto explore his own potential. He discovered that he loved writing. He contributed a piece to the student newspaper, *Forty Acres and a Mule*, and its publication gave his self-esteem a life-changing boost.

Forty Acres and a Mule gave voice to the inner realities of the young people at the Prep. Its managing editor, Cyril James, wrote:

> "The sensitive, perceptive young writers are mature beyond their years, and their maturity manifests itself in their poetry—the brash, the funny, and the subtle.

> The colloquial used here, you will no doubt understand. However, the details of the picture they paint of the world around them as well as within them, you may not recognize.

> When the unfamiliar is used to make a very profound and familiar point (to you), here lies art."[131]

One student could hear the sounds of his native Puerto Rico and feel the memories they evoked even deep in the cold New York City winter:

> *The air is cold and still, nothing but the piercing*
> *Winter wind can be heard blowing right thru the*
> *Heavy coats and freezing the flesh*
> *Now and then the rapid, staccato footsteps of a*
> *Passer-by resound through the empty streets.*
>
> *But listen more deeply now!*
> *Listen with your heart and with your eyes tightly*
> *Shut, and then you will begin to hear.*
> *The heavy throbbing murmur of the congas, maracas, and drums,*
> *Compelling you, begging you to come.*
>
> *The scratchy whispers of the guicharos (gourds), the*
> *Plaintive sounds of claves (sticks) clapping together*
> *And you hear the warm sea breezes.*
> *Suddenly, echoing all around you are laughing, happy*
> *Voices of jibaro (country) music, urging you to*
> *Dance, to join in the fun.*

You open your eyes—but there is only the dark
Night sky and gloomy shadows through which you again
Feel the cold wind.

But now there are distinct sounds, sounds of coffee
Perculating and sights of small children as they peer
Through frosty window panes.
All around is yearning, the hopes of cold hundled
People, praying for a warm island of green ...
Puerto Rico"[32]

Another student expressed the emerging 'black consciousness' of many students through a new interest in African roots:

"From Brother to Brother

Hey there black man

Where do you roam?

Do you not knoweth

Africa is your home?

I was born in America,

Raised on Harlem's streets.

I have never been to Africa.

Of what nonsense do you speak?

Your real great grandparents

About ten generations back

On the red soils of Africa

Lived in huts of mud and thatch

What proof have you?

Were you not there?

There are not only blackmen in Africa

But you find them everywhere.

As I was about to say

Before you rudely intervened

One day the white man came

To corrupt the peaceful scene

He intended not to stay

But it's a known fact

He kidnapped your grandparents

And planned to take them back

To the thirteen British colonies

And many stops on the way

That's why you can find blackmen

Around the world today

So you are an African

Be respected as a man

Not as a Negro

But Afro-A-merican."[133]

For almost all students—except those who would go on annual trips with "Dr. Ben", the African history teacher—Africa was more mystery than reality:

"Ghana

To the Afro-American it's a mystery

But very important in his history,

For before America he couldn't trace

The exact origin of his race.

    Land of great wealth

    Land of great health

    Land of great Gods

    Land where beauty clods.

But of ignorance it's the truth

That's why slavery was its youth

And still today to my surprise

The African black neglect to rise,

But regardless, it's still our home

No matter where on earth we roam."

Poems also described both the outer world, in which the students lived and moved, and its inner realities. One student voiced the pain felt by the chronic challenge of keeping a family together in a difficult environment:

"Daddy

Daddy, Daddy, Daddy dear

Where were you in time of fear?

Where were you when Ma was sick?

Out in the street thinking you're slick.

Tell me why you left me Pa?

Oh, the Lady had a brand new car.

Did you ever think what might become of me

While you were out swinging from tree to tree?

Remember that time you came in drunk?

I remember your breath it really stunk.

By the way, May didn't get the monthly check.

Oh, the Lady's new car, you were in a wreck.

Ma, who's in bed with you?

I've never seen him before.

Oh, that's your new daddy son,

Now close the door."[134]

The reality of daily life in Harlem was called into question:

"Harlem

Harlem how proud you look from these hills so far

But Harlem, how deceitful you really are …

…I know

For I have lived in you, and I know the hell

You perpetuate there, that tortures a man for having woolly hair …

But Harlem I know your Smell

Of stagnant life suffocating from dreams locked in a barless jail

I hear your sounds

Of armed night, stabbing, the woman at 122nd St., pushing her

Frightened eyes down, bumping steps, purse gone

Young women screaming, hollering through streets, clothes torn

And sounds only dope addicts make, skin-punctured quiet

Where dope keeps heads nodding, backs bending

And sounds of uneducating schools teaching

The unworking and underpaid, bitching

Searching for a full table, and the good, good life they say

Harlem I see dollars of a million

People in three and a half square miles, stream

Pains of economic racism drinking their blood like a giant leech
…"[135]

Through Harlem Prep Alberto Cappas escaped the limitations of his neighborhood. He and his friends all went to college where he became president of the Hispanic Student Union at the University of Buffalo and his friend and fellow Prepper, Murray Parsons, founded the Black Student Union. Murray wrote at the time: "The foremost of my conceived realities is the guiding factor that can be applied to myself and my race. That is that before a man can question the authoritarians he must himself first attain a position of authority."[136] Alberto included much of his learning from Harlem Prep in "The Pledge", a statement of right thought and action which he used to help others:

"I pledge to maintain a healthy mind and body

Staying away from the evil of drugs

I pledge always to try my best to understand the importance of knowledge and education

Painting a positive picture of where I plan to be tomorrow

Not allowing obstacles to stop the growth of my plans for the future

I pledge to seek answers to questions

Understanding that the answers to questions always lead to other discoveries

I pledge to work hard

With the awareness and confidence that the hard work today

Will serve as the seeds for my strong tree tomorrow

A tree that no one will ever be able to tear down

I pledge to learn proper languages, beginning with the language of my mother

Always prepared to appreciate others

I pledge to gain a better understanding of myself, by understanding my cultural roots

To fully accept who I am as a human being

A rainbow of many cultures and colors

I pledge to overcome any personal misfortunes

Becoming stronger from such misfortunes

Always striving to become a wise person."[137]

5 ~ First Graduates

Harlem Prep was the viable way forward for many young people who had struggled not only in the public system, but also in their families, in their neighborhoods.

The Urban League's 'street academies', small storefront schools founded in the mid-60's that functioned outside the public system founded in the mid-60s, were bearing fruit. Academies had now been started in the lower East Side, Brooklyn, and the Bronx. They took in "dropouts" and "force-outs" and prepared them for high school, college, and jobs training programs.[138] In the public system, a "mini-school" movement had developed in which a very small school was developed out of a much larger school and operated somewhat autonomously within the public school. The large Haaren High School was sub-divided into fourteen semi-autonomous mini-schools.[139] The New York Urban Coalition and McGraw-Hill partnered to start the Harambee School which was connected to Charles Evans High School, a poorly-performing high school on the lower West Side. Wingate Prep was begun with help from Pfizer Inc., in connection with Wingate High School in Brooklyn. These efforts were replicated in other American cities.[140]

And by the early 1970s, Harlem Prep had made it.

Under a bright June sun, the Carpenters, Ahdieh, MacFarlane, and all the Harlem Prep the teachers sat in front of the Adam Clayton Powell State Building on 125th Street in Harlem to graduate the new class.

In the class of 1970 yearbook, the teachers offered these wishes to the graduates:

"Hoping you will seek higher elevations through knowledge. Move to self-esteem and personal dignity. John M. Minors, Mathematics Teacher

I urge the kind of training and development which will contribute to the Black Community through experiment and self-determination. J. Clayton Flowers, Vice-Principal

Wishing that the students coming from Harlem Prep will show a new leadership role to mankind and especially to your communities. George Simmonds, African-Studies Instructor

To the Harlem Prep students who are "moving right along" – In college you have a multiple choice for the use of your hands: with them you can: a) reach out, b) clench, c) write and type, d) touch, e) beckon, and f) hurt. In every "test", choose wisely and with heart. Sister Liz, English teacher

Best of luck to all! Especially: Sophia Carlisle, Michele Warren, Willie Pope, George Clayborne. You four will need all the luck you can get. Connie Vinson and Tonya."

Graduation

The more formal 1960s had given way to the individualism of the 1970s. Students had gone from dark blue blazers and pleated skirts to broad lapels and wide ties, big collars and light summer dresses. The American flag hung on a pole to the side instead of being carried by a student. The "Moja Logo" flag stood to the back of the staff who faced the students. Now, the enthusiasm of the students students was expressed without restraint. They laughed and smiled and celebrated each other's accomplishments out in the open on Harlem's central street. One young man in a blue-cream, three-piece suit, crossed the dais to receive his award while another in a green suit and black bow tie and shades smiled. Dressed in brown and sitting under a parasol, jazz composer Valerie Capers—the first blind composer to graduate from the Julliard School of Music—played the electric piano.

Mike Longo, pianist for Dizzy Gillespie's band

Dressed in a brown suit with white lined breast pockets and sporting fashionable sideburns, Ahdieh acknowledged from the lectern individuals who had supported the school. Charles Rangel was the newly elected Congressman for Harlem, having unseated the long-time incumbent, Adam Clayton Powell Jr. He was beginning what would become a very long and distinguished career in the House of Representatives. He knew well the lives of these Harlem Prep students: he had grown up in similar circumstances and seeing how far these young people had progressed astonished him. He had only learned that he had capacity when he became an expert in artillery in the army and earned a Purple Heart for bravery. Throughout his public career he would support alternative movements to poor public education while advocating for constructive dialogue between different educational efforts and for the advancement of the teaching profession.[141] Carl McAll had been a teacher, had become an ordained minister, and was now serving as a State Senator for the Harlem district. He had been backed for office by Percy Sutton, a former Freedom Rider and lawyer for Malcolm X, who was the highest ranking black official in the City, serving as the Borough President of Manhattan, a position he would hold longer than anyone else. Watching the proceedings was Irving Anker, the Superintendent of the public schools of New York City. He was in the middle of overseeing the decentralization of the Board of Education structure into locally controlled districts in response to the many concerns raised around school integration, the quality of education in minority neighborhoods, and the desire for self-determination. The ceremony was undoubtedly a respite for him from the bruising politics of New York City—the task of decentralization was fraught with challenges. Harlem Prep was an example of a way forward.

Congressman Charles Rangel receiving award for his support of
Harlem Prep

"For the first time, for most of us, we became a family of learners
giving and taking each other's worth as essential to our own
growth. We grew out of our learning from each other whether we
agreed or not. We hung onto the words of each speaker, teacher or
student. We questioned. We tested. We challenged. We questioned
some more. We were building our capacity to be teachers and
learners. We brought to the table what we had come to know, what
our experiences and circumstances had taught us. We brought our
suspicions and our prejudices. We brought our single mindedness.
And gradually, we brought faith, hope, and trust. We were Jewish,
Christian, Muslim, Baha'i. We were atheist, True Believers or not.
We were Five Percenters. We were black, white, brown and tan.
We were Harlemites. We were African, African-American,
European, Caribbean, Iranian, Puerto Rican and we were
Dominican. We were protective and supportive of each other. We

were family, and, together, we spoke success." (Sandy Campbell, teacher, Harlem Prep)

Naledi Raspberry arrived at Harlem Prep in 1970 barely older than her students. She had been working at an ad agency that had her figuring out ways to entice more black people to smoke, but she wanted to find something more meaningful to do. At her Harlem Prep interview, Ed Carpenter asked her what she wanted to see in the world. This school without walls, with its transformational agenda and impassioned teachers attracted her. After teaching summer school, she began in the fall.

What she found was a world much tougher than any she had known. She had graduated from the elite Vassar College and had grown up in a secure neighborhood in Kansas City. Here at Harlem Prep she encountered a place where school and life went together. Because she taught English and Drama, she encouraged students to draw on their own life experiences. In one class, she had a girl who had become pregnant but couldn't afford maternity clothes so she came to school in larger and larger t-shirts; the man who had impregnated her did not contribute any money. The other students, seeing her plight, snuck into her house—which was quite rundown—and painted it. This generosity was paid for a by a local drug dealer who moved large amounts of money. Naledi attempted to talk with him about the harmful consequences of his work because, fundamentally, he was a generous person.

Ed Carpenter would not tolerate any drug dealing in the school—nor would the students. Once, he had to rescue a dealer because the students were dragging him downstairs to throw him out. In addition to the obvious harm the drug dealers caused, their presence cast the school in a bad light and, as an experimental school which challenged the mainstream educational system, this could hurt the its chances of survival.

Naledi found her students to be reading well below grade level—some as low as the fifth-grade. Many of them did not believe in themselves so she looked for ways to engage them from "where they were at" she. She knew she was making progress as a teacher when her students stopped pushing the dividers back to listen to the dynamic math teacher nearby instead of her.

She had a drama class in which she used exercises that she had learned at the nearby National Black Theater which she had joined. She suggested that the students write a play together. This brought out powerful stories of their real lives which gave an emotional dimension to the class and moved everyone deeply. The students also received free admission to the National Black Theater, exposing them to live acting. Naledi and her students went from the school to her apartment where she made them chili and then on to the theater.

In her English class, she had them write a research paper on a topic of their interest. In addition to learning the basics of writing, the students also experienced doing research out in the world. To help them learn punctuation, she had them do free writing which they then reviewed for punctuation. She was mentored by Mrs. Panyagua, became like her older sister at the school. They were able to collaborate easily because the teachers' desks were along the walls of the main room. Mrs. Panyagua assured her that once her students felt safe and had succeeded at a task, they would be able to build on that experience.

Naledi was one of the favorite teachers of Judith Barton.[1] Uninspired at Erasmus Hall High School in Brooklyn, Judith had begun skipping classes. She went to visit Harlem Prep without her mother knowing after hearing about it from acquaintances and was very attracted by the exciting, open atmosphere. She fit right in at the Prep. Here was a school that gave its students freedom of self-expression while expecting mature behavior in return. Students knew they were having a special experience and were always willing to collaborate as well as hold each other accountable. As a side benefit, she and other students got jobs at the black-owned MacDonald's on 125th St. which recruited at the Prep. The restaurant was near the Apollo Theater so the young teenagers met some of their favorite singers such as the Unifics and Black Ivory who came in for food. For graduation, she wore a lovely African-print dress from the Ashanti Bazaar. The ceremony exemplified the self-respect and freedom of expression that had been her experience at the Prep. Inspired by Naledi, she went on to study journalism and became a writer.

---

[1] Judith goes by Maitefa Anganza today.

85

In another class, Naledi invited her students to imagine that they were participants in a revolution—because revolution was in the air and on their minds.

Stokely Carmichael, a prominent activist in the Student Nonviolent Coordinating Committee and, later, the Black Panther Party, sent someone to speak at the school. The Black Panther Party was a black nationalist organization that initially was focused on patrolling the streets against police brutality in black neighborhoods. This brought the Panthers into conflict with law enforcement officials, and the FBI monitored its activities. When Party members were killed, the prestige of the Panthers increased in the eyes of the community because this validated the claims of police brutality. Its community service activities—such as its free breakfast and health care programs—also boosted the respect in which they were held by many black Americans. The year 1970 marked its peak year of membership. Their militancy and ideology appealed greatly to some of the young men at Harlem Prep who had experienced their community's challenges.

Revolutionary poets were everywhere. Sonia Sanchez, a poet deeply concerned with the inner lives and relationships of black Americans, was pulled in to speak to students when she happened to be nearby. She knew well of the aspirations of black Americans:

"we are sudden stars
you and i exploding in
our blue black skins"[142]

Islam was a growing religion in the black community in these years. Phenize Abdur-Rahim had grown up in a Christian family but then converted to Sunni Islam. He and his friends called themselves the "men of truth". This was a time when many young people were searching spiritually and politically. The friends had worked together on a newspaper and become attracted its Islamic ideas. They were encouraged to read the Qur'an and, after doing so, they converted. Harlem Prep was perfect for a young seeker like Phenize. Going there for the first time was one of the best days of his life. Its non-standard structure and approach to education, the warmth of the Carpenters, and the dedication of the sisters, appealed to him, as did the perception of the school's "anti-establishment" stance. He felt challenged and inspired by this dynamic learning community made up of people of different philosophies. His two best friends, Umar and Dumar, belonged to a more radical form of homegrown Islam, the Five Percenters, related to the larger Nation of Islam.

The Nation of Islam may well have been the most influential of any single group among the students. With roots in the black neighborhoods of Detroit—especially poor migrants from the South,— the Nation attracted people with its message of lifting up the black race, its condemnation of the Bible and its white followers, and its use of the Qur'an as the true spiritual guide for the black man and woman. The teaching was popularized by Elijah Muhammad who proclaimed himself a Prophet and founded many mosques. The Nation of Islam's stark emphasis on a religious and apocalyptic interpretation of the racial conflict in the United Sates held a powerful appeal for young people because of the stridency of its message, its call to righteousness, and its very clear stand in a time of turmoil and change. It strongly opposed all white institutions which, to many young black people, were the true authors of the suffering in their communities and called on black people to arise and find their true selves outside of the established order:

> "He (i.e. the founder of the Nation of Islam) declared that we were without the knowledge of self or anyone else. How we had been made blind, deaf and dumb by this white race of people and how we must return to our people, our God and His religion of peace (Islam), the religion of the prophets. We must give up the slave names of our slave-masters and accept the name of Allah (God) or one of His divine attributes. He also taught us to give up all evil doings and practices and do righteousness or be destroyed from the face of the earth. He taught us that the slave-masters had taught us to eat the wrong food and that this wrong food is the cause of our sickness and short span of life. He declared that he would heal us and set us in heaven at once, if we would submit to Him."[143]

Several students at Harlem Prep were active members of the "Five-Percenters", a group founded by a former member of the Nation of Islam. Its name derives from the belief that 10% of people on earth control the other 85% and only 5% know the real truth. In this belief system, the Black Man and Woman were the fathers and mothers of all on earth and, therefore, the "Gods" of humanity. This especially exclusive self-identity and appeal to secret knowledge may well have attracted some of the young men at Harlem Prep. Female teachers, such as Naledi, and female students struggled with this group's lack of acceptance of women as equals to men and thought that this belief system allowed its male followers to do as they pleased.

For Judith Partelow, another very new teacher female teacher, the world from which these students came was entirely foreign to her. She had been teaching at a middle school in Pennsylvania after earning her degree in Secondary Education/English and had recently become a Baha'i. She had heard of the Faith several times and then, again, from an actor on a boat trip back from Europe. He introduced her to other Baha'is. The first gathering which she attended was in the home of an inter-racial couple. She was swept away by the vision of a unified future and declared herself a Baha'i. This brought her into contact with a young activist white priest who lived among black Americans. He excited her about working for the betterment of society. Soon they were married and both became involved in the Baha'i community. She heard of Harlem Prep through the Baha'is. There, for the first time in her life, she had real interactions with black Americans. She experienced true fellowship in the Harlem Prep community, sitting around tables with students, freely exchanging ideas, and receiving the support of her colleagues. One day, Ed Carpenter even provided her with funds after her money had been stolen. She thrived in what was for her a new environment of inter-racial cooperation and action and came to believe completely in the mission of educating young people.

"I have lost all doubts about going to college. I know what it will take for me as an individual to get there" James Christenberry Davis. Student, Harlem Prep

Harlem Prep encouraged discussion among students. For many, the conversations themselves were the learning experience. Ed Carpenter insisted that all exchanges be respectful and so, despite their strong ideological differences, the students developed a genuine appreciation for one another through sincere dialogue. This dynamic of vigorous open debate within the school's supportive family-like environment remained one of the most enduring features of Harlem Prep in the memories of those who went there.

School assembly

The school's large open space and sliding dividers allowed for all-school assemblies which were the perfect venue for a dynamic exchange of ideas. The dividers were pushed to the side, and students clustered around the tables. Some sat forward, following the presentation intensely, others sat back looking skeptical, most waited to engage the speaker and each other. The Assemblies were lively. William Buckley, the preeminent conservative intellectual at the time, who had a real impact on American politics as a writer, editor of *The Nation*, and public speaker, espoused views which were diametrically opposite to those held by many in the student body. In the ensuing question and answer period, the students experienced in Buckley someone who really stuck to his positons even while being faced with a critical audience. From the other end of the political spectrum, Julius Lester also spoke to the students. He was beginning an extraordinarily prolific career as a writer, teacher, photographer—he took many photos of the Student Nonviolent Coordinating Committee—and recording artist. Lester also hosted a radio show on WBAI. His orientation was to try and create understanding between people of different backgrounds while working for social justice. He did not favor the militancy increasingly expressed by young black Americans. During the Assembly, he was vigorously challenged by students. Assemblies were also occasions for great cultural enrichment. One day the main room was completely re-arranged to make room for pianist Billy Taylor. Visiting a school to speak to young people and inspire them about music was a natural activity for Taylor who, in addition to his tremendous talents as a jazz pianist, became a learned spokesman for the art and an educator about its history and innovations.

These assemblies, discussions, and free periods, and countless informal interactions made Harlem Prep a very exciting place to be for Debbie Reeves, who was at the very beginning of her professional life when she joined the staff. She had heard through her aunt that the school was looking for an administrative assistant position and was soon assisting the school secretary. Even though the job could be quite chaotic, she loved coming to work. The students were only a little younger than she was—and were positive, and she enjoyed speaking with them on their way in and out of the building. A sense of unity and purpose pervaded everyone there, whatever their roles. She made good friends among the teachers including one science teacher who claimed astrological knowledge. She read Reeves's hand and predicted future events which actually came to pass. Ann Carpenter—with whom she interacted a great deal—provided stability.

The school was a place of constant interaction between teachers and students—MacFarlane and Ahdieh speaking with a group of visiting students, a teacher in the media area demonstrating a technical point, a student explaining his vision for his art piece, a math teacher—chalk in hand—going over a point with a group of students close by soaking it in …

Ann Carpenter and other teachers guided a young Eric Williams through his schooling. He had grown up in a family that was in turmoil, and his life was characterized by instability. At Haaren High School he had known Ann Carpenter, head of the English Department there, Gary Hilton, head of the Science Department, and Barbara James, a guidance counsellor. Haaren seemed to Eric to be a dead-end both socially and scholastically. He could not relate to his peers who were from a very different background. He was interested in science, technology, and film but all the school's equipment was out of date. The curriculum was preparing them for jobs that did not exist. Gary Hilton introduced Eric to television production which opened his eyes to this as a possible career. The school, though, was hopelessly behind the times. The times were changing rapidly, and Eric was a part of an inter-racial group of friends interested in contemporary politics and music. As a young black man, he thought nothing of listening to popular white musicians like the Rolling Stones, as well as being interested in issues of black consciousness. He expressed much of his interest in writing.

Dr. Ann Carpenter and Bd. of Ed. Chancellor Ankar at graduation

Finally the gap between the public high school and the dynamic world outside became too great and Eric dropped out. He lived with hippies and went to rock festivals, got high, and hitch-hiked to anti-war demonstrations; his cousins had come back from the war permanently damaged.

Still, he stayed in touch with some of the Haaren teachers, though Ann Carpenter and Gary Hilton had moved on to the Prep. He didn't know how to take the next step—college. An open, flexible, and dynamic school like Harlem Prep seemed like an answer, especially since Ann and Gary Hilton now worked there. At the Prep, he still felt out place over issues of identity. The decade had seen a broad questioning among young black Americans about identity—what it meant to "be black". Some young people developed flexible self-concepts while others were much more doctrinaire and wanted very clear definitions of "blackness". Eric found a real friend in a fellow student nicknamed "Bingy" who was a handsome Jamaican and with whom he could hang out and listen to WPLJ and Jimi Hendrix kissing the sky.

Other young men were radicalized.

Keith Williams had attended St. Aloysius School on 132nd Street but by the 3rd grade the nuns thought the school was no longer the right fit for him. He was becoming defiant. So he was transferred to PS 168, where he experienced gut level Harlem street life for the first time. He was placed in the intellectually gifted program both in that school and the next public school he attended. He wound up at the prestigious Stuyvesant High School. Soon, Keith was skipping classes and becoming socially conscious and attracted to the Panther party, gradually becoming influenced by its ideas. His mother was heartbroken. His sister, who had struggled, now attended Harlem Prep where she shone, and he followed her into the Prep in 1971. Having come from such structured environments, the Prep's relaxed environment shocked him. Harlem Prep did expect a measure of personal self-discipline, as the Prep's loose structure, though, demanded of personal self-discipline from any students who wished to graduate from it. Like other students, the greatest revelation he experienced there was to learn about African History from Mr. Smith.

Cliff Jacobs had also attended Catholic schools. He had studied at Cardinal Hayes High School but began to clash with school authorities. He had gone through the Archbishop's Leadership project, which was originally designed to train young black men for the priesthood, and included training in manners and leadership. The program included reading a book a month, going on retreats, and learning to eat at a formal table. But he got into trouble for putting up posters of Malcolm X and Huey Newton. He also wrote an essay questioning the Church's involvement in South Africa which was written from the heart and shocked his teacher who then kept it and used it against him at a disciplinary hearing.

Cliff had a questioning nature. He was a third-generation Harlemite and wondered why his neighborhood was so different from those south of 110th Street. He became aware of the Black Panther Party and was influenced by Existential philosophy, which led him to want to take his life into his own hands and leave Harlem. Upon his first visit to Harlem Prep, he decided to go there. He entered in the '72-'73 school year and excelled. He didn't have to suffer the racism of his previous school and was greatly influenced by the English teachers Sandy Campbell and Caroline Humphries. His life opened up significantly when he won an essay contest sponsored by CBS and the World Youth Forum, by which he and eight other students were awarded travel to Paris, Switzerland, and England. He and fellow Harlem Prep student, Dawn Mitchell, were the two black American students in the group. In Europe he learned that prejudice against black people was not universal. Now that he knew otherwise, he could let go of that idea and be free of its grip. His time at Harlem Prep reached fruition when he got into eight of the ten schools to which he had applied and was the valedictorian of his graduating class at Harlem Prep. He ended up on a three-quarters scholarship to the prestigious Brown University. Later, he would return to Harlem to study at Ossie Davis' Institute New Cinema Arts (INCA) which had been established by Ossie Davis—himself a booster for Harlem Prep—to help black people get jobs behind the camera in film and television.

Kimberleigh Manley came to Harlem Prep from a conservative background. Her father worked two jobs; she knew he was home when she saw his work clothes in the hamper. Both of her parents wanted to shield their children from the "black realities", especially those of lower-income life. The children were sent to white Christian schools. When it came time for high school, Kimberley found classes Walton High School boring and irrelevant. Her mother was horrified by what went on in the public schools and took her to Harlem Prep. Kimberley entered the Prep as a sophomore. She was amazed to find that everyone wanted to learn. She became hungry for knowledge herself, looking forward to going to school every day. Here, she could explore her own thoughts freely. She went on school trips to museums such as the Planetarium, even going to the Natural History Museum with her friends on her own. She went up to City College to take in Earth, Wind, and Fire, at the free Music Festival and got interested in jazz— Billy Taylor, Dizzie Gillespie, Phyllis Hyman. She was a cheerleader on the pep squad. The teachers energized her. She loved studying music with Arnold Jones and learning about biology from Martha Manley. Her parents insisted that she must choose college, the armed services, or the work world. She was accepted to Fordham University and Ohio State on scholarships. She knew how much Harlem Prep, and especially Ann and Ed Carpenter and MacFarlane, had been her parents away from home and given their all for the students. They were saving lives—including her own—without even knowing it.

☼

"The Free School press and Free School writers speak more often of Bill Ayers' Free School, in Ann Arbor, which did not work out, than they do of Edward Carpenter's remarkable and long-sustained success of Harlem Prep. I have said in an earlier section that I have a great deal of respect and admiration for Bill Ayers. Still, it cannot be easily bypassed or ignored that, insofar as the Free Schools are concerned, Bill Ayers' experience is perhaps the very prototype of the Eloquent Exercise in Self-defeat. I believe we can and ought to honor people like Bill Ayers. In the same way, many of us love and revere the name of Che Guevara. There is also Fidel, however, who was not afraid to sit within the victor's chair, and there are also strong and able people like Ed Carpenter. It would not hurt us to have upon the walls or in the stairways of our little schools not only photographs of those who do not fear to die for their beliefs, but also photographs of those who do not fear to win."[144]
(Jonathan Kozol, Educational Reformer)

Emerging educational alternatives such as Harlem Prep pulled on the straight-jacket in which American public education was bound. In the late 20th century, the United States had the finest 19th century educational system in the world. The new free schools engaged in much needed experimentation and out-of-the-box thinking. Such schools allowed a student to derive meaning from sense-making experience in the broader context of where humanity was going. In such a setting, young people could become self-aware and see that they could take charge of their own development and, as a consequence, the evolution of society.

Education had been governed largely by tradition and opinion. The new alternatives were taking a fresh look at curriculum, classroom structure, and staffing, and searching for new definitions and new models.

Such alternatives were doubly necessary for black students from low income backgrounds who were caught in a cycle of low expectations and academically impoverished schools. White teachers who believed that these students could accomplish little, sent the message that only certain jobs or futures were open to them and that they should be content with the trajectory followed by previous generations. Discouraged from excelling, black students struggled to consolidate an identity that could help them achieve. To be effective, white teachers would have to be aware of this important reality of black children.

Higher-education institutions began to get behind the effort to innovate in education. One of those was the University of Massachusetts at Amherst which hired educational reformer Dwight Allen, a tenured professor of education at Stanford University specializing in teacher training, to head its School of Education. The University's Provost thought the school had become out of date. Allen agreed to accept the position on the condition that he could make many new hires to counter-balance the number of tenured professors and that these hires could be people from a variety of fields so as to create an inter-disciplinary school of education. As a result, the School of Education soon counted lawyers, physicists, and sociologists among its teaching staff, giving it much greater breadth and potential to be innovative. Allen had a genius for bringing people together and giving them the space and time to learn and grow. The school now attracted a greater variety of students. These included Ed Carpenter and Hussein Ahdieh who completed PhDs at the university's School of Education during the early '70s while they were managing Harlem Prep.[145]

Another student to enter this program was William "Smitty" Smith. The youngest in his family, he got off to a rocky start in life, eventually being sent to reform school where he met many troubled young people. He remembered a boyhood friend named "Boom Boom" in his neighborhood who was gifted in math but whose life was cut short by gun violence. Fortunately, Smitty was able to turn his life around. He served as a medic in the Vietnam War and got involved in civil rights activities, working for the Black Awareness Coordinating Committee of South Carolina. He and other young Baha'is were actively engaged in increasingly radical activities. The Baha'i institutions helped them to channel their passion for justice into productive and spiritually-based actions that rejected both violence and separatism.

Through these interactions with Baha'i institutions, Smitty met Dwight Allen. The love he felt from the Baha'is helped him to grow beyond anger. He entered the University of Massachusetts to pursue film and education—he had a special interest in those whose troubled lives echoed his own youth. The Ford Foundation was investing greatly in education at the time. Through the University, Smitty received a grant from the Foundation to go to Harlem Prep, which he had heard about from a Baha'i friend. His purpose was to "shadow" Carpenter to learn about alternative education.

Smitty found an important role model in Ed Carpenter: a black man who carried himself with confidence and could move effectively in the white world while still remaining grounded in the context of the black community. Ed was a can-do man who often retorted, "How do we figure this out, how do we do this?" For one year, Smitty followed him through his busy, high speed, super-charged days of faculty and business meetings, learning about operations and structure. Smitty was struck by the faculty and administration's outlook which was, "Yes, we can", and the belief that lives could be improved. At Harlem Prep, he made friends for life. When Smitty decided to marry, Ann Carpenter helped smooth over the relations between Smitty's black family and his bride's white relatives. In time, the families grew to genuinely love one another.

Smitty completed his PhD and went on to found his own highly successful alternative school in Massachusetts, the Springfield Street Academy, which included a vocational program. He used some of Ed Carpenter's arguments and approaches in raising funds for his school. One of the most meaningful pieces of recognition he received was a plaque of appreciation from Harlem Prep. He would treasure that symbol of recognition because the Prep helped him get started in life.

Ed Carpenter was the beacon that kept the vision of Harlem Prep lit, motivating people to follow a dream. His charisma brought people together. On crazy days when the school became more like a three-ring circus, he was the ringmaster. Ann Carpenter provided the steady management that such a school requires. Hussein and MacFarlane troubleshot problems every day and in every way to find solutions to difficulties as they arose. The staff labored dedicatedly to lovingly guide the students. But Harlem Prep always had the quality of "moreness"— the school was more than the sum of its parts and personalities.

To put the rocket ship that was Harlem Prep into space took a great deal of effort and sacrifice. To keep it up there would require something that came to be in short supply as the plentiful '60s and its idealism turned into the depressed and tougher reality of the '70s: money.

6 ~ Financial Stress

1970 was a year of fruition and growing pains for Harlem Prep. The school now could stand on its own and no longer required the mooring of the New York Urban League. Callender and Ifill ended their service at Harlem Prep. The Sisters from Manhattanville College, who had done so much to erect Harlem Prep and staff it, ended their period of service there. In June, 1970, its charter was renewed for another three years. Funding for the school came from over fifty private sources, the highest number it would ever reach. Corporations also provided human resources in the form of tutors.

Robert Kingsley, Manager of Urban Affairs for the Exxon (Esso) Corporation was active in supporting the school. Paul Austin, CEO of Coca-Cola, who turned the drink into a giant international brand, also believed in the Prep. The Mosler Foundation, IBM, Chase, the Port Authority, and Metro Life Insurance, all made important one-time grants. Ed Carpenter and Ahdieh made frequent in person appeals for funding at various organizations. To help convince donors of the value of the school, students were often invited to meetings as examples of the school's success. Jonathan Kozol encouraged the use the student's voice in making plain an alternative school's needs:

"Their job (i.e. students) is precisely to break down the bureaucratic walls and secretarial defenses that surround these foundation officers. They also join the teachers and the parents in the actual confrontation. Harlem Prep and several other schools in other cities do it in this manner also. It tends to transform the entire atmosphere within the corporation office, as well as to shake up the ordinary state of mind of those who work within it."[146]

Ed Carpenter and Harvey Spears with Exxon CEO

Despite the efforts of Carpenter and Ahdieh and the goodwill of many people and organizations, the realities of the great downturn of the American economy in the '70s and corporate restrictions on giving could not be avoided.

New York City was especially hard hit.

Ominous portends had already been seen in the 60s. There was a population shift to the suburbs. Traditional manufacturing disappeared. There were strikes by labor unions. The Brooklyn Navy Yards were shut down. The 70s recession exacerbated this downward trend. The huge subway system came to be seen as both unreliable and unsafe. Times Square—the most visible public space in New York City—was a tawdry mix of drug dealers and sex for sale. Homeless people moved into abandoned buildings. Central Park at night was feared by many. City revenues were dropping but public expenditures kept rising. When Mayor Beame went to seek federal help, President Ford turned him down resulting in the next day's headlines: "Ford to City: Drop Dead".

The largesse of 60s idealism was shrinking. Corporations were willing to give seed money, but not to fund initiatives indefinitely.[147] Sooner or later Harlem Prep would have to find a permanent solution to the financial shortfall— the school could not survive on aspirations alone. An article in *The New York Times* described its challenge:

"Harlem Prep, the private, tuition-free high school situated in a renovated Harlem supermarket, is in financial trouble—again.

"In the past," said Ann Carpenter, the school's director of curriculum, "consumers and stockholders pressured corporations to pay their dues, to justify their existence to the black community by supporting our school."

"But these efforts were not sustained," she said, "The nobility of the act has died out."

Harlem Preparatory School, its proper name, has had to cut its projected 1972-1973 budget by one third—-from $600,000 to $400,000. Nine instructors will be let go; remaining faculty members will take a 10 percent pay cut and 10 full-time teachers will be used only part-time.

Promises not fulfilled

Edward F. Carpenter, Harlem's Prep's headmaster and Mrs. Carpenter's husband, said a fund-raiser supplied by one of the corporations had estimated earlier this year that the school would have a certain income.

"But this did not materialize," Mr. Carpenter explained. "The monthly projected income was based on promises that were not fulfilled."

In an interview at the school at Eighth Avenue and 136th Street, Mrs. Carpenter said that the school was in trouble until next fall. The Federal funds and possibly City Board of Education money will be available in major proportions.

Currently, the school receives Federal Upward Bound money and funds for the 12 per cent of its students who are war veterans.

Mrs. Carpenter noted that the school's cost was about $900 to $1,000. This, she said, is below the city's comparative costs for specialized high schools, and below the Upward Bound figure, which is $1,440 per student per year.

Mrs. Carpenter said the school had been a success since it opened in the fall of 1967. It has sent 476 graduates, many considered castoffs of the public school system, on to many of the nation's best colleges.

One graduate is beginning his training as a physician at the Mayo Clinic; five or six graduates are in the Ivy Leagues, and four graduates completed their college work, graduated, and returned to the prep to teach.

Success has not spoiled the school, but success may kill it, Mrs. Carpenter said. The foundations that supported the school in its early years are reluctant to continue.

"The foundations supported us for one or two years," she said, "but they say they are interested in experiments, in demonstrating what can be done for our type of students."

She said Harlem Prep had been a "model for 2,000 such schools in the nation."

Mrs. Carpenter said that she sensed "a feeling of envy, a dissatisfaction that the ones [students] who were creeping and crawling are now standing on their own two feet.

"Liberals and conservatives can't deal with the idea. It is a subtle threat to the Establishment and to the powers that we could put our graduates into colleges to rub shoulders with their children."

Mr. Carpenter, the headmaster, said that the school had "knocked down every stereotype that it has about black and Spanish students not being able to achieve, about black and Spanish parents not being interested in their children, about the kinds of homes needed to produce college students—about such things as having books in the home, about white teachers coming into Harlem to work and about what we can learn from each other."

Central Harlem has no public high school. The only other high school in that community is the 34-year old Rice High School, at 74 West 124th Street, a predominantly white Catholic institution.

The faculty and administrators of Harlem Prep hope to collect on some of the unfulfilled corporate promises.

The community, Mrs. Carpenter said, has given its "complete moral support" and she said also that "there is not a single social club in Harlem that hasn't supported" the school financially.

"But they could do more," said Hussein Ahdieh, assistant administrator.

"Yes," Mrs. Carpenter added, "Many persons equate publicity with support."[148]

The school cost about $40,000 a month to run. In 1970, there were 176 students enrolled and the waiting list was over 2,000 names, but increased admissions depended on more funds. The school had already graduated a remarkable diversity of individuals including a forty-nine year old grandmother, a mother of four trying to get off welfare, and a night clerk who was becoming a pre-med at Fordham, among many others.[149]

The street academies were also in financial peril. Ominously, Newark Prep, the Urban League's flagship high school, had run out of money and closed its doors. The New York Urban League itself was $750,000 in debt—unbeknownst to many of its funders and Board members. Corporate donors asserted that they had done their part by funding academies for their first two "startup" years. Dr. Callender answered that social change could not happen that fast. Pan-American Airlines claimed that it had been hit hard by the recession and so it had to retrench. Chase Manhattan was re-directing its $2.5 million "urban affairs" budget into minority training, loans, and projects other than street academies. Some corporate donors had experienced first year disappointments with projects in which monies were paid out, but the schools had either no real students or else a highly fluid student body. In other cases, there were cost overruns and neglect in construction: materials that were paid for and then disappeared, architectural plans that were overly ambitious and did not conform to existing codes, and written reports that were promised but not produced. The six major corporate supporters of the street academies had also justified ongoing funding to their shareholders by describing the thrust of these efforts as being "institutional change" of public schools, but as time went on it became clear that the thrust was much more about "remedial education"[150]

Overall, these schools suffered from inexperienced financial management, and this lack of administrative expertise made corporate donors skittish. In urging continued support for the academies, and Harlem Prep in particular, *The New York Times* summarized the challenges for the street academies and the Prep:

"Although the recession is responsible for drying up some sources of funds, alarming lapses in educational leadership and fiscal management have also eroded the confidence that is so crucial to their success. At issue is not only slipshod accounting; far more basic is the question whether a combination of uncertain goals and inadequate professionalism has jeopardized the educational mission itself.

Collapse of these experiments would be particularly heartbreaking in the case of Harlem Prep, which, more than the Street Academies, started out with clearly defined objectives and an able faculty. Its early record of grooming for college many youngsters who had been virtually written off by the public education system became a significant demonstration of a possible cure for the educational pathology of urban slums.

The resignation of the academically most expert members of governing board and staff earlier this year indicated that the developing malaise had deeper causes than the admittedly serious fiscal crisis. But the death of either or both of these experiments – Harlem Prep and Street Academies—would set back those vital attempts to create new models which might eventually be adopted by public mass-education. It would be the end of a dream for many youngsters.

It is not enough to say that this must not be allowed to happen. The original hopes can be recaptured only through an unsentimental recognition of the need of expert academic supervision and instruction, competent administration and efficient as well as honest book-keeping.

These are absolute requirements for success. If they are met, the services and cooperation of many of the original supporters and advisors who still feel deep affection for the projects could be re-enlisted. None of these steps imply disenchantment with orthodoxy. But nothing could be more destructive than the romantic notion that fiscal and academic quality control may be suspended when the future of disadvantaged young people is at stake. Such double standards, in addition to being condescending and discriminatory, will shut off the flow of funds. For both reasons, immediate reforms are essential not as a penalty for past misdeeds but to assume future support and success."[151]

While the Prep's freewheeling, experimental atmosphere may have unsettled some of its more staid observers, and its administrative challenges may have made donors cautious, it was still held in great respect and had not been tainted by the accusations of fiscal malfeasance which had been made about other similar schools. It remained a very viable candidate for corporate and government donors. Though Harlem Prep was not technically a "black school", the majority of its students were black American young men. The economic numbers showing that black Americans remained well-behind white Americans in economic and educational indicators despite the gains of the 1960s buttressed the argument for continued support of the school; for example, in the early '70s one third of black Americans lived below the poverty level, while only nine % of white Americans did, and black students were still far more likely to dropout than their white counterparts, though the dropout rate was declining.[152]

With such public interest, friends of Harlem Prep organized private fundraisers. Richard Feigen opened his art gallery at 27 E. 79th St., for the first one. Mrs. Feigen organized the benefit which was co-chaired by Mayor Charles Evers the older brother of Medgar Evers, and the first black mayor of a Mississippi town since Reconstruction, and Mrs. Lindsay, the wife of the Mayor. The occasion for the evening was an exhibit, "Dubuffet and the anti-culture", of the art of the innovative French artist, Jean Dubuffet. The tickets for the exhibition were $30-$50. Handwritten notes were also sent to sell $100 sponsor tickets which were bought by William S. Paley, the chief executive of CBS; Judith and Samuel Peabody, generous philanthropists who supported the Dance Theater of Harlem among many other projects and causes; Nathan Cummings, the Canadian founder of the Sara Lee Company and philanthropist; Jackie Robinson, the legendary baseball player who broke the color barrier; Herman Badillo, the first Puerto Rican Congressman of the Bronx and Bronx Borough President; Mary Lasker, whose husband, Albert, was considered the founder of modern advertising; and Chicago realtor, Arthur Rubloff. Members of the Harlem Prep Benefit Committee were made up of prominent New Yorkers interested in education, modern art, civil rights, and liberal politics. They included Mrs. Theodore Kheel, a Board member of the New York Urban League and wife of the famous labor mediator who had resolved the major newspaper strike in New York City in the early '60s, and Mrs. Alfred R. Stern, vice-president of the board of the Northside Center for Child Development, a mental health clinic serving Harlem families.

Feigen wanted his art gallery and openings used for socially important causes:

> "I've made a policy decision to take on nothing that does not have social or political implications. I don't want any of these social butterflies around me. We are in a revolutionary condition. If a symphony doesn't open, we won't have a holocaust. But if we raise $10,000 for Harlem Prep with this show, it will make a difference. It could be 5% of their budget."[153]

Corporations stepped up as well. In March of 1971, Standard Oil stepped up to infuse funds into Harlem Prep to prevent its closing. Clifton C. Gavin Jr., vice-president of the company, announced that it would be providing $100,000 for the current year so that the students could graduat,e and another $150,000 for the operation of the school over the next few years. Although much more money would be needed, the school breathed a sigh of relief and could continue for the time being. The new president of the school's Board, Judge Robert Mangum, noted from experience: "So many things in the last 35 years I've seen in this community have failed. We need a success."[154]

Hussein with Judge Robert Mangum

Aissatou Bey-Grecia's love for the arts developed in part from her mother's opera singing, and the times inculcated in her a desire for activism. As a little girl she grew up in a segregated neighborhood in which her mother could not pursue her operatic career. Aissatou[2] had experienced the Detroit riots, triggered by a police raid on an unlicensed bar, which spiraled into the second most destructive race riots in American history after the Draft riots in New York City during the Civil War. Her family moved to New York City. She enrolled in Music and Arts High School near City College, a campus ablaze with black power and anti-war fervor. The black community was trying to "find itself"—and so was young Aissatou. Different worlds co-existed within her. Raised on classical music, she listened to Jimi Hendrix. She played bass violin while learning African dance. At Music and Arts she met the daughter of famed South African singer Miriam Makeba, and Yuri Kuchimara, Malcolm X's close friend. She gravitated towards dance as her main form of expression.

---

[2] Formerly Sherry Sims.

Music and Arts had few black students, and she felt that the "Harlem kids" were not especially welcome, as though the school's quality was being lessened by having them there. She left that school to attend the Lincoln Academy on 133rd Street, one of the street academies in Harlem. College was her mother's main hope for her, but she was too young to go when graduation came, so she enrolled there.

She became an active participant in the Prep's African Dance Troupe that had been begun in mid-October of 1969. In 1970, the troupe included Barbara Murphy, Debbie Reynolds, Debbie Epps, Paula Allen, and Madonna Thorton, among others. More than any other activity, this one gave her a sense of empowerment. She had already begun to study in the Olatunji dance program that was being offered in Harlem. The dancers were invested in performing authentic African dance. Their repertoire included "Funga", the welcoming dance of the Yoruba tribe of Nigeria, as well as "Boot Dance and Yarbo Dance". They even went to a Dutch trader on the lower East Side who sold authentic cloth with which they could make their own outfits. The lead drummer was Jerry Wooley, joined by Charles Simmons, Larry Jones Malik, Floyd Hollington, and Ray Richards. Ed Carpenter was proud of this accomplished group of young people and frequently presented the troupe to visitors. The dancers were helpful in inspiring contributions to the school.[155]

Education became a tool to further Aissatou's activism—what she was learning had to be useful for her future and to greater causes. At the Prep, she found an atmosphere in which she not only encountered very different points of view, but these views could be openly debated without fracturing relationships. The airing of disagreements was important in and of itself. This atmosphere was dynamic but also safe because the teachers were coming from a good place and cared enough to call students on something they would say--there was a raw accountability. Aissatou interacted with "Five-Percenters", white Catholic nuns, Persians, Baha'is, returning war veterans, and teachers of different ages. These encounters made everyone think more deeply about issues. Every day was an exciting and enriching experience. By the time Aissatou got to college, she had already had most of the important conversations.

Nicky Wilson also participated in the dance troupe. She commuted to Harlem Prep from Queens where she grew up in a college-educated family. Her ambition was to go to Hampton Institute in Virginia, one of the top historically black universities in the country.

Harlem Prep to her wasn't just a "right-on" school. Students engaged in frank discussions that went beyond simple external categories. The school introduced students to life outside the black experience as well. The open structure of the classroom allowed students to jump into arguments that were going on in other classes. One student asked her in the middle of an exchange, "What do you think?", to which she replied, "I'm not even in the class". While Harlem Prep was academic, some students were not in the standard sense of the word. They were more street-wise than book smart, and they brought that experience to the life of the school. Students were outspoken and articulate, ready to move and shake, and proud to be at Harlem Prep. The businesses in the area were also proud to have the school in their midst and felt a sense of ownership about it.

Nicky knew from the very first visit to the Prep that she had to go there. Ed Carpenter helped to guide her, and the curriculum allowed her to follow her interests. The whole experience bolstered her self-confidence, and by graduation she was ready. That same day she received her letter of acceptance to Hampton University.

Josie Alvarez joined the dance group, but in her case the experience was practically traumatic as she had no sense of rhythm. This encapsulated much of her experience of being an outsider. Previously, she had always been the only black student in class because she had been bussed to school. Now at the Prep, she managed to gather together her own group of friends. The school also showed her the road to college. Once at Loyola, her fellow black students asked her in surprise, "You went to school with black folks?"

Sherry Kilgore lived across the street from Aissatou and heard her rave about Harlem Prep—little did she know that her uncle Ed was its head. Though she was a good student, she could no longer go to traditional schools because she had a child. Once at the Prep, she was shy about students knowing that Ed Carpenter was her uncle because she felt everyone might scrutinize her. Carpenter, though, looked after her and held her accountable. The school was a safe and welcoming enough environment, so much so that she could bring her son; other students had similar situations. If she needed help with her child, someone always stepped up. Harlem Prep's learning environment helped her to grow out of her partying lifestyle to being engaged in the issues of the day. She enjoyed organizing anti-war protests and participating in lively debates. This greater seriousness of purpose helped guide her into becoming an entrepreneur in her professional life and her son a lifelong learner.

"It is recognized that education is the key to free the underprivileged from slum housing, poor health, unemployment and poverty. Educational iniquities handicap the poor, and especially minority youth. Deprivation at home, inadequate school facilities and intolerable factors of environments force many of these young people most in need of educational opportunities to leave school prematurely.

The Harlem Preparatory School was founded five years ago to meet these very problems. ...

Inasmuch as the modest tuition charges do not meet the needs of the Harlem Preparatory School, the churches of Harlem, along with business, civic, social and fraternal organizations of the community, have set aside one day to offer full support to the young men and women of the school.

Now, therefore, I Nelson A. Rockefeller, Governor of the State of New York, do hereby proclaim the day of Sunday, May 2st, 1972" to be Harlem Prep day."(Declaration of Harlem Prep Day, State of New York)

Actor Ossie Davis stood at the lectern on the west side of Seventh Ave. between 124th and 125th Streets. He spoke to the 3,000 students, family members, supporters, and onlookers, about the importance of the black community supporting Harlem Prep with the same commitment that it gave to its churches. He had just participated in a major fundraiser for the school at Lincoln Center titled "$urvival" with Sammy Davis Jr. headlining and including Melba Moore and the Isley Brothers, among many others. Dressed in a dashiki, Wayan (Balar) Powell gave an impassioned student welcome:

> "We are the young and we are the future. We have to show the younger ones that we are successful black people and are unified. We are all growing greatly. And all the young who come to see us here will join with us to build the black community."

The Moja Logo school chorus sang with soul, backed by a nine-piece R and B rock band, Zebra. The student awards followed one after the other, each applauded enthusiastically by the crowd: the Sojourner Truth Certificate for Service, the W.E.B. DuBois Certificates for Academic Achievement, the Malcolm X Certificate for Perseverance, the Alibizu Campos Certificate for Inspiration to All, the Victor Gomez Certificate. Then Moja Logo and Zebra kicked in with the school song "Keep on Marching":

"Keep On Marching

Step by step
You're in the race at Harlem Prep,
For the race has just begun,
There's a goal for everyone

Open those gates,
Open them wide
For those who hunger and thirst inside,
For the creative free
Who once were denied.
Keep on Marching
Until you reach the other side

Through the halls of opportunity
To the stairway of success.
Work you show
You're on the go.
Just keep those students coming through,
For there's so much work for us to do.
With the help of God and the hand of fate
We'll make our dream come alive
No matter what it takes
No matter what it takes
No matter what it takes
No matter what it takes"

Sammy Davis Jr. at Harlem Prep

Pete Seeger, supporter of Harlem Prep

Bayard Rustin, supporter of Martin Luther King Jr. and organizer of March on Washington

Charles E. F. Millard, president of the Coca-Cola Bottling Company of New York and a trustee of the school, re-assured listeners that the school's financial strains would be relieved. The coming year's budget had a shortfall of $150,000 to 200,000. Millard promised "to accept this challenge—to do anything necessary to see to it Harlem Prep stays open." Standard Oil, local businesses, and individuals, made the same vow; Jersey Standard hired a professional fundraiser to assist the school.

A capable Board of Trustees would try to end the year-to-year chronic shortage of funding which held the school back from further development. The tall and distinguished president of the Board, Judge Robert Mangum, had a long record of public service. He had often been the first black American appointed to a particular senior position—he was a trailblazer though not a radical. His success had been hard won and fraught with difficulty, but he was always modest about it. He took his share of criticism for being a black man who was part of a system which was seen by many as inherently racist and possibly irredeemable. Having earned a law degree from Brooklyn College, he had been the Deputy Police Commissioner in charge of the Juvenile Aids Bureau, appointed the Deputy Commissioner of Hospitals by Mayor Wagner, served as the New York State Commissioner for Human Rights, and had been elevated to Judge in the Circuit Court of Claims. In 1963 he had founded "One Hundred Black Men Inc. of New York City" which he, plus future mayor of New York City David Dinkins, and businessman J. Bruce Llewellyn, to have a positive impact on the black community. This initiative attracted other members such as famed lawyer Johnnie Cochran; actor and comedian, Bill Cosby; Manhattan Borough President Percy Sutton; Congressman Charles Rangel; and attorney Gregory Meeks, among others.

Serving with Judge Mangum on the Board were Harold Dicks and Russell Goings. Goings was a Renaissance man. He had been raised in poverty but managed to make it to Xavier University in Ohio, with the assistance of a caring guidance counsellor who had helped him with his dyslexia. Before University he served in the Air Force and also trained in martial arts in Japan. From martial arts and Xavier's Jesuit tradition—both of which he admired—he learned self-discipline. He excelled in football and played professionally for the Saskatchewan Rough Riders of the Canadian Football League. He had a successful stint there but had a career-ending injury before he could join the Buffalo Bills in the more prestigious NFL. He decided to become a stockbroker, an unusual choice because it was a career which seemed to hold no future for black men. He got a position, though, at J. W. Kaufmann & Co. in New York and realized that there was a business opportunity in the increasing number of successful black entertainers, athletes, and businessmen. businessmen. He invested in black-owned ventures such as *Essence* magazine. Eventually he founded First Harlem Securities and bought a seat on the New York Stock Exchange, becoming the second African-American-owned business to do so.[156]

Harlem Prep had reached an initial stage of maturity, and so, in January of 1973, this Board petitioned the Regents of the University of the State of New York for a permanent charter. The school had functioned under two three-year provisional charters since its founding in 1967. In its petition, the Board highlighted some of the schools successes: 477 graduates had been placed in colleges, the curriculum had been expanded to further meet the students' needs, students were being referred to the Prep from a wide variety of schools beyond the original street academies, and the number of colleges accepting graduates had increased greatly. Despite the school's success, its challenges in the area of funding would ultimately cause this petition to be rejected.

ᘓ

"We have done so much with so little for so long that now we can do anything with nothing at all."

(*Konstantin Josef Jireček, Czech historian, Harlem Prep proverb*)

ᘓ

With funding from a foundation, the school hired the Institute for Educational Development in early 1973 to evaluate Harlem Prep, a necessary step in the life of any school. The site visits were made by two experienced educators: Robert Atmore, the head of the Choate School, a coeducational boarding school in Connecticut with a reputation for academic rigor, and Henry Drewry, the head of Princeton University's Office of Teacher Preparation and Placement.

Their report was a snapshot of Harlem Prep and where it had been.

The first graduating class had been overwhelmingly male—thirty-five male students to five female students. Over the next few years the male-female ratio closed to 2-1. By the time of graduation, most students were between nineteen and twenty years old and, by 1971, about two-thirds of the students travelled from outside Manhattan. Most had done very well in school until the 8th grade; their real school problems became evident in 10th grade. The average student spent two semesters at the Prep, enough to complete the degree needed to be able to apply to college. The variety of colleges accepting Prep students broadened to include schools in the South and West. The number of students had increased from over one hundred to over four hundred. The tallying of attendance was stringent—students had to attend all their classes to be considered 'present' during a school day; the Prep had about a 20% absentee rate on any given day. The cost of educating a student remained around $1,500 per year. The twenty-five teachers on staff were mostly new to the profession; nine had advanced degrees.

The evaluators agreed that Harlem Prep was a unique institution with a clearly defined purpose. They felt welcome in the school and were struck by the friendly atmosphere and lack of suspicion towards their visits. They described the tone of the environment as "gentle, yet militant" though the school was conservative academically. School decisions were guided by student need. The administrators acted as leaders and while they maintained warm, open relationships with students, they were not "buddies". Roy Ahdieh, Hussein's brother and a teacher at Harlem Prep, described the student teacher relationship:

> "It seems to me that students are more friendly. You see, in a regular school, the teachers are in one group and the students are in another one. But here, it is the other way around. Most of the time, the teachers are among the students... We want to be among the students and the students are all the time free to come any place that we are."[157]

This contrasted with his teaching experience in Iran:

> "In a way, it's easier to teach in Iran. Once the teacher, as I said, is going to start teaching, the students are silent; they take their notes; he gives their homework and he goes out. That's all he does. But here, you have to be responsible for lots of things...It's not just a test that you give every month."[158]

The report found that students had a sense of ownership towards the school as evidenced by the lack of vandalism, theft, or graffiti. Roy noted that students learned responsibility from freedom:

> "The majority of them like it, but sometimes, some of the students tell us that we've given them too much freedom. What we reply to them is that they've got to learn to act when they are free. It's not all the time there is a teacher on top of their heads to check on them. They have to be able to study when there is nobody to supervise them."[159]

In class, the students were not "psychologically absent"—a common phenomenon in other schools. Because they were free to leave and voted with their feet, the students who were in class were fully engaged; sometimes, students sat in on a class even if they were not enrolled in it, simply because they were interested in the discussion. The teachers were totally dedicated and competent. They tended to be conservative in their methodology with little use of role-playing or inductive teaching. More teacher-training, especially peer to peer, would have improved the teaching of the less experienced staff. The fact that few teachers wrote formal lesson plans may have inhibited their professional development. Teachers taught four courses with an average class size of fifteen, though this was smaller in the science classes.

Though there was a specific guidance counsellor, guidance itself was an ongoing practice in the school because students had open and constant communication with the faculty members. The guidance office then could be more loosely structured with students able to walk in spontaneously to get help rather than having to make a formal appointment. In their feedback to the evaluators, students appreciated the "family" atmosphere of the school and the freedom to learn and felt overwhelmingly positive about being there.

The weakest aspect of the school, according to the report, was the poor record-keeping, attributed to a lack of resources. Similarly, the science rooms, the library, and music department, all needed much development. A full-time librarian who could teach research skills was sorely missing. A gym would also have been a great benefit, especially for the boys for whom activity was a physical imperative.

In considering the future of the school, the evaluators expressed concern about Harlem Prep being absorbed into the public school system. In a large bureaucratic structure, the school would lose the distinctive qualities that had made it successful. This possibility loomed larger as the school's financial crisis continued to grow.

The 1972-73 school year was again a financially stressful one. Some programs had to be phased out just to make it to the end of the year. The school administrators were clearly frustrated by the lack of response to the thirty-three funding proposals submitted to the Federal Government:

"No one can tell us what we've done wrong. Consultants have told us the proposals are fine, and that it's a matter of time before we get some assistance. But, for us, time is running out."[160]

The staff and faculty were asked to take a 10% pay cut, and nine instructors were let go. There was a sense that because this school had been successful in showing dropouts could be educated, it was no longer necessary—it had "made its point". This strange logic, according to Dorothy Taylor, assistant to the headmaster, might account for the loss of funding:

> "Many people feel it's no longer fashionable to support us now that we're no longer new and innovative. Now that we've proved that so-called uneducatables can perform on the college levels, supporters are concluding that the noble experiment is over.[161]

The school kept operating in expectation of receiving a $150,000 grant from the Ford Foundation. Joshua Smith was the program officer responsible for the Harlem Prep portfolio at the Foundation. He could recommend grants and then supervise the successful ones. The Prep approached the Foundation every year for money. He remembered his first site visit because his mother died that day. When he first walked in, he looked up at the high ceiling and the blue cigarette smoke rising up, and thought to himself, "Wait, this is a school?" He grew to love the place with its charismatic leader and caring faculty and enjoyed the site visits.

In attempting to keep the school going financially, he worked closely with Judge Mangum who became his mentor. They lived near one another and met at a local restaurant where they spent afternoons trying to come up with solutions for the school. They tried to get more money from Exxon, but this source dried up. Despite their best efforts, they could not get the Prep on a sounder financial footing. Among other things, the school lacked political muscle—someone who could work the financial system and government for funding. Smith left the Foundation for a distinguished career in educational administration. As the new Dean of the School of Education at City College, he was confronted by another full-on financial crisis during which he had to work hard to save minority jobs. As the President of the Borough of Manhattan College, he had to help the school weather an accreditation scandal. He often drew on the expertise of Judge Mangum to help him with expert advice and professional connections. Both men shared the experience of being the only black person in senior administrative positions.

To help meet the financial shortfall, another large fundraiser, "An Evening with a Dream", was held in April, 1973, at the Felt Forum/Madison Square Garden, headlined by Bill Cosby, Herbie Mann, David Ruffin, and others. The letter written by a student enclosed in the event's invitation tells of the anxiety that many at the Prep were feeling:

> "No one would sit and watch its child die. Harlem Prep is only a child and it belongs to the world.

> IF WE SHOULD DIE

> I cringe to think what would happen if we should die. If for one moment the heart of Harlem Prep should stop beating, for me the sun would never rise again. If we should dies a beautiful family would no longer exist, and our hopes to help our country and world would cease.

> We at the Prep have never thought of dying because a family that has loved together and cried together could never think of death. We have experienced inside the walls of Harlem Prep all the emotions and moods which characterize the love relationship of a family. ...

> We are now in the midst of our most severe crisis in a short life filled with crises. If Harlem Prep should die, one more dream will be broken in a community that can't stand any more broken dreams. If we should die, it will mean a loss for my child, your child, and the children of the world. ..."[162]

7 ~ Final Efforts

"Harlem Prep, the tuition-free school with a reputation for turning high-school dropouts into college graduates, will not reopen this fall unless the Board of Education agrees to take it over, the school's leading trustee said yesterday."[163] (*The New York Times, 1973*)

The yearly drum beat warning of Harlem Prep's possible closing due to lack of funds had grown much louder by the summer of 1973. Judge Mangum saw a takeover by the public system as the only option for saving the school which was now going from paycheck to paycheck. There were numerous legal issues involved with bringing the school under the NYC Board of Education: teacher certification, the planning of curriculum, student attendance, and zoning. Several of Harlem Prep's most talented teachers did not have the certifications which the unions would insist on them having if the school became part of the Board of Education. The Exxon Corporation through Mr. Roser was providing most of the funding for the school by this point.

Many enthusiastic supporters of the school's experimental nature were apprehensive about a Board of Education takeover. They feared that Harlem Prep would lose its uniqueness and become simply another school, that would be in a curricular and pedagogical lockstep with the rest of the city's schools. There was great concern among Harlemites about the public school system:

"I grew up in Harlem—I know much about the problems of its youth. The public schools have not been able to educate any of them with success. But here is a school which has had no failure. We desperately hope to continue but, if taken over by the city, we still need the latitude in teacher selection and curriculum that has given Harlem Prep its outstanding accomplishments."[164]

Judge Mangum's feelings were echoed by the co-chair of the Harlem Parents Union:

"There's something devastatingly wrong with the city schools. Something has to be done. They put children in a box. They all come out alike. I feel my tax money is wasted. But I completely trust what Harlem Prep is doing. They run the school with the conviction that the kids can make it."[165]

Like many others, the co-chair hoped that the Board of Education would allow the school to continue to be independent, all while supporting it financially:

"I think the state should allocate money to Harlem Prep so that it can carry on its present program independent of the city school system. I wouldn't like to see it in the grip of bureaucrats."[166]

Despite Judge Mangum and the Board's best efforts, more financial support did not materialize in time. When students came to school for the opening of the 1973-74 school year, the doors were closed. The *Amsterdam News* announced in a headline, "Harlem Prep Dies for Lack of Funds".

In its editorial page, James Hickes penned an especially strong polemic about the situation making use of strident language and imagery from the late 1960's:

"Three hundred Black teenagers were quietly murdered in a long dark tunnel in Harlem last Monday at the hands of some of the most respected people in New York City.

They met death in the most cruel way one can imagine.

They were not shot. They were not knifed. They were slowly strangled to death at the hands of persons unknown.... The murder victims of whom I speak are the Black teenage dropouts, who, until last Monday were crawling like moles through a long dark tunnel called Harlem Prep. They were the student body at Harlem Prep.

The "Establishment" people had told them that if they crawled through the tunnel to the light which they could see at the end of the tunnel, they would have a "second chance" at living the Good Life like everybody else.... But suddenly last Monday, the light at the end of the tunnel went out. Someone had slammed a mighty door at the end of the tunnel and placed a padlock on it marked

"Closed".... The respected hands which closed and padlocked the Harlem Prep door——the hands which committed the actual murder——will not be revealed.... They belonged, instead, to a living body called "The Establishment"——a name which covers a multitude of sins in our society—including murder."[167]

That fall, Ed Carpenter, Judge Mangum and the Harlem Prep Board, State Senators, the NYC Board of Education's Office of Planning and Research and Personnel Department, and Exxon were all trying to find a way forward.[168]

The school was able to open, but Ed Carpenter had to inform several hundred hopeful applicants that the school would not be able to enroll any new students.[169] Then on November 22nd, School Chancellor Irving Anker held a news conference to announce that he would propose to the Board of Education that it transfer Harlem Prep to the public school system. Ed Carpenter was present but felt disheartened by the coming change.[170] There were doubts in many peoples' minds about the possibility of maintaining the school's unique character. Officials from the Board of Education conveyed confidence that Harlem Prep could maintain some independence while abiding by its rules and regulations. Central among these rules were the requirement that all teachers be certified—few teachers at the Prep were, and even Ed Carpenter did not have an official city principal's license.[171] In addition, there would be stricter age requirements preventing anyone twenty-one years or older from attending. Students at the Prep didn't care about any of this: "We have teachers here who aren't certified. But they care, and that's what makes Harlem Pre unique."[172] Another student summarized the feeling of his fellow students about the public system: "They're really jive. They put students through a lot of hassles."[173]

This concern was shared by members of the Harlem Prep Board including Frank O'Shea. O'Shea was a junior officer at Chase which he had joined right after school. He had grown up in an Irish Catholic family of modest means and was accustomed to working hard. His sister had gone into a religious order, and his parish priest suggested he consider the priesthood, so it was a natural fit for him to serve on Chase's philanthropic sub-committee. The Rockefellers were major shareholders in the bank and insisted on corporate tithing. O'Shea was also interested in the use of money for social development; in his career, he came to see firsthand the corrosive effects that too much money could have on people. Chase had made a multi-year commitment to Harlem Prep, and the school became part of his portfolio. He evaluated projects that were pitched to the bank, a task which made good use of his analytic skills in determining which projects could make it. In addition to Harlem Prep, he worked with an off-off Broadway theater company. The school had no stable source of funding, and he struggled with Judge Mangum to come up with a permanent solution. Giving these projects half of the needed funding was of no use—it was all or nothing. The school needed to be completely solvent to be able to function at all.

O'Shea made regular trips to Harlem. This was his first time in a black American environment; all of the schools he had attended and his workplace were almost completely white. He was able to learn from the experience because he had been reared in an open-minded family. At the Prep, he found people—students and staff—who thought outside the box. Though many of the students had formerly been written off, he could see they had real street smarts. The passion shown by Ed and Ann Carpenter for the mission to help lower-income young people inspired him—later in his life he would serve on school boards in Glenn Rock, New Jersey, and at the prestigious international school in Djakarta, Indonesia.

Much of his time was spent in interfacing with the IRS because the school owed money due to having used tax money to help itself stay open. He knew Harlem Prep was out of money, and that only a transition to the public system could save it.

Harlem Prep did not have a strong advocate inside the NYC Board of Education nor any significant political muscle which could protect it in the coming absorption. Another educational project, "City as school", a school that stressed experiential learning through internships, was able to keep its distinctive approach because it had connections with former District superintendents who were able to protect its distinctiveness; the "City as school" model was replicated in other cities.

Al Lofti witnessed the transition from an independent Harlem Prep to the NYC Board of Education Harlem Prep. He arrived there in 1974 by accident. He had been teaching at Benjamin Franklin High School in Queens, but had to be re-assigned because of budget cuts. The

Board of Education re-assigned sent him to Harlem Prep. He was shocked when he first came to the school and saw its open configuration. He couldn't believe a school without walls but soon found that it was a fun place to be. He became accustomed to got used to students drifting in and out of classes. Though the teachers had few resources, he enjoyed creating his own classes. Lofti was taking Dr. Ben's position who was leaving Harlem Prep. He taught international relations because it interested a group of students; another semester he taught government and spent much time getting the students registered to vote. For the first time, he experienced students bringing their own small children to school when they could not find anyone to look after them.

The student body was more diverse than any he had ever known. Some students were over twenty-one—the legal limit for the official rules of the NYC Board of Education. Some had served in Vietnam—one had contracted malaria—another was in her sixties and trying to get her high school diploma, while others had no life experience whatsoever.

He found a dynamic and diverse faculty. Cecil Clark was an English teacher who was very streetwise and the students from a similar background related to him. His boyhood friend had become a cop who would stop by and check-in on the school to see if they needed help with troublemakers—disruptive people showing up at school was a normal occurrence. Hector Julietti was a much loved, middle-aged French teacher who had gone to college on the GI Bill and had come from Harlem High, an experimental school that modelled itself on Harlem Prep but had been hit by budget cuts. Nick Mbumba, a native of Namibia, taught math. After several years of teaching, he disappeared. His Ghanaean wife was frantic to find him. He had returned to Namibia to become involved in the political struggle there and later became one of the heads of SWAPO, the ruling party of that country.

Lofti could see when he was out and about the neighborhood the people were very proud of the school. Often when he and other teachers went across the street to Maxy's for lunch, customers offered to pick up their tab.

He experienced the transition of Harlem Prep. Chancellor Anker was eager to save the school. There were two overall issues when transitioning from a completely independent school to a public high school in the official category of "Independent Alternative High School" within the structure of the NYC Board of Education the status of the staff members and the building.

As of 1974, only three Harlem Prep teachers had regular teaching licenses. All staff would have to get their licenses to be able to be employed by the Board of Education at Harlem Prep. They were issued temporary "Certificates of Competency" but would have to complete course work and sit for tests in a timely manner. Over the next years, the professional standing of the teachers was regularized. Because of Board of Education rules regarding seniority, salaries, tenure, and union rules, each employee at Harlem Prep had to be categorized on a particular grade. Mangum felt strongly on this issue when it came to the title of the category into which Ed Carpenter fell. By the Board of Education and union rules, Carpenter went from being "Headmaster" to "Director" when the Board of Ed took over, then "Head", then, because of the rules of advancement, "Assistant to (Administration). Carpenter and other administrators had never had the 'lower professional grades', so they could not simply be placed in the higher grades. Judge Mangum wrote to the Chancellor that this was insulting to a person of Carpenter's accomplishments and would be seen as such by the community. These kinds of bureaucratic issues gave the staff the sense of being harassed.

The success of Harlem Prep meant that the redesigned supermarket was no longer a viable site for the school. The Board of Trustees was legally its owner, and it leased the building to the NYC Board of Education. There were serious fire violations because of a lack of a sprinkler system that would require significant funds to install. The lack of space and the size of the student body meant that programs important to the school's growth could not be developed. For these reasons, the Trustees wanted to sell the building but found it difficult to find a buyer. Finally a buyer—a supermarket—offered to purchase the building in February, 1978. A new and larger home would have to be found for the Prep. Mangum and the Board of Education went back and forth about different locations. Schools in the district were being consolidated, freeing up space, and new buildings were being built. Mangum requested that JHS 120 be considered, but the Chancellor responded that the building had been severely vandalized. Another alternative that was considered was PS 149. Unable to agree on a new location, the Trustees and the Board continued on a month to month lease. Finally, IS 201, on East 126th St., was decided on as the new location. The school had been the epicenter of the struggle for community control of schools in the '60s during the decentralization by the Board of Education.

Al Lofti remembered the move as a difficult one. The Prep was allotted only one truck for the move. The new, modern building to which it was re-located turned out to be a climate controlled prison with traditional classrooms. The students of the Prep shared the building with two other, poorly run, schools. The bells didn't work and all the clocks told different times, resulting in uneven dismissals for which teachers were reprimanded. Because of the school's location on the east side, the students from central Harlem were reluctant to venture out of their comfort zone.

Ann Carpenter bravely directed the school during this transition and tried to save as much as she could. Some staff members felt that the NYC Board of Education didn't actually want a school like Harlem Prep around because its success had been an indictment of the public-school system. In IS 201, the remainder of Harlem Prep's uniqueness disappeared. The original vision met a bureaucratic death.

"Without education, you're not going anywhere in this world" (Malcolm X)[174]

Afterword ~ Harlem Prep's Legacy

The search for meaningful reform of the public school system, which included the creation of alternatives within the system, grew from the experiments born in the creative turbulence of the 1960s. Though many of these experiments died out in the 70s because the private funding for them dried up, new types of public schools emerged. Also, a plethora of private schools with very different philosophies of education and often radically re-structured classrooms and school days, emerged as well but, of course, were limited to families with the means to pay the often high tuition.

By the first decade of the Twenty-First Century, there were over 10,000 district-administered public alternative schools to help at-risk students.[175] In the 1990s a charter school movement began to challenge the main public system by creating free public schools that would operate independently under the provisions of a charter and be free of certain constraints imposed on the regular public school. Twenty years later there were almost 6,000 charter schools operating in the United States—5% of all public schools.[176] Another option—magnet schools—were more embedded in the public system. Such schools had a particular focus and could attract students from across the regular public school's geographic boundaries—possibly helping to desegregate districts while not imposing bussing. By the turn of the century, there were over 3,000 magnet schools in the United States.[177]

Among the ancestors of these thousands of schools were places like Harlem Prep.

The lettering has come down from the old supermarket on Eighth Avenue. The whole building has received a white coat of paint with a row of international flags planted along its roof and has been dedicated to the worship of God. While time moves on, neighborhoods change, people die and are born, the spirit of those years at the Prep animates the idealism of today and the future through its story, its influence, its educational DNA passed down through society's genes.

Most of all, Harlem Prep was ordinary people from different backgrounds and with different beliefs, all laboring together side by side—both hands on the plow—for something greater than themselves, for the common good: to educate young people who might have otherwise been left behind.

Notes

[1] Rev. Eugene S. Callender, Nobody if a nobody: the story of a Harlem ministry hard at work to change America, self-published, 2012, 10

[2] Callender, Nobody if a nobody, 33

[3] Gilbert Osofsky, Harlem: The Making of a Ghetto, Negro New York, 1890-1930, (Chicago, IL: Elephant paperbacks, 1966), 144

[4] Osofsky, Harlem: The Making of a Ghetto, 76-95

[5] Ibid, 17-24

[6] 128

[7] 136

[8] 140

[9] 146

[10] Nancy J. Weiss, Whitney M. Young, Jr., and the Struggle for Civil Rights, (Princeton, NJ: Princeton U. Press, 1989) 13-14

[11] Weiss, Whitney M. Young, Jr., 46

[12] Ibid, 52

[13] 57

[14] 73

[15] 73

[16] 4

[17] John A. Andrew III, Lyndon Johnson and the Great Society, (Chicago, IL: Ivan R. Dee, 1998), 14

[18] Andrew III, Lyndon Johnson and the Great Society, 13

[19] Ibid, 22

[20] 92

[21] 23

[22] 26

[23] 27

[24] 28

[25] 27

[26] 38

[27] 44

[28] 46

[29] James Baldwin, "Fifth Avenue, uptown", Esquire, July, 1960, 70, http://www.esquire.com/features/fifth-avenue-uptown

[30] Fred C. Shapiro and James W. Sullivan, Race riots, New York, (NY, NY: Crowell, 1964)

[31] Capeci, Dominic J., The Harlem Riot of 1943. (Philadelphia, PA: Temple University Press, 1977) 101

[32] Peter Goldman, The Death and Life of Malcolm X, (U. of Illinois Press, 1979) 57

[33] "Mangum, Robert J.", retrieved 2/27/15 from:
http://www.encyclopedia.com/article-1G2-2509911737/mangum-robert-j.html

[34] Kenneth B. Clark, Dark Ghetto, (NY, NY: Harper Collins Publishers, 1967) 57

[35] Bennett Harrison, Thomas Vietorisz, The Economic Development of Harlem, (NY: NY: Praeger Publishers, 1970), 9

[36] Alphonso Pinkney, Roger R. Woock, Poverty and Politics in Harlem, New Haven, CT: College and University Press, 1970), 28-9

[37] Harrison, Vietorisz, The Economic Development of Harlem, 11

[38] Clark, Dark Ghetto, 30

[39] Harrison, Vietorisz, The Economic Development of Harlem, 11; Pinkney, Woock, Poverty and Politics in Harlem, 29

[40] Harrison, Vietorisz, 37-8

[41] Clark, Dark Ghetto, 34-5, 37-9

[42] Harrison, Vietorisz, The Economic Development of Harlem, 21-2

[43] Pinkeny, Woock, Poverty and Politics in Harlem, 36

[44] Ibid, 30

[45] Harrison, Vietorisz, The Economic Development of Harlem, 32

[46] Clark, Dark Ghetto, 113-4

[47] Ibid, 118

[48] 124-5

[49] 90

[50] 84

[51] Pinkeny, Woock, Poverty and Politics in Harlem, 32

[52] Clark, Dark Ghetto, xxii

[53] Ibid, 12

[54] Pinkeny, Woock, Poverty and Politics in Harlem, 23

[55] Ibid, 21-24

[56] Richard Sevdro, "Kenneth Clark, Who Fought Segregation, Dies", New York Times, May 2, 2005
http://www.nytimes.com/2005/05/02/nyregion/02clark.html?pagewanted=1&_r=2)

[57] Charles Kenney, No Ordinary Life, (Public Affairs, NY: NY, 2012) xiv-5

[58] Kennedy, David M., Freedom from Fear: The American People in Depression and War, 1929-1945. (Oxford University Press: Oxford UK 1999) 232

[59] Kenney, No Ordinary Life, 7-16

[60] Religious of the Sacred Heart of Jesus, "Who we are", retrieved November 4, 2014 http://rscjinternational.org/who

[61] Religious of the Sacred Heart of Jesus, "History", retrieved November 4, 2014 http://rscjinternational.org/who/history

[62] Manhattanville College, "History", http://www.mville.edu/about/history.html retrieved November 5, 2014

[63] Harlem Prep application to the Board of Regents, July, 1967.

[64] "Ruth Dowd, R.S.C.J. '40: Risk Taker, Visionary", Making a difference, January, 2010, 15)

[65] Ruth Dowd, Manhattanville: From Harlem to Here, Manhattanville Alumnae Review, Summer, 1968, 5

[66] Ibid, 15.

[67] Ruth Dowd, Manhattanville: From Harlem to Here, Manhattanville Alumnae Review, Summer, 1968, 4.

[68] Letter from Dr. Terino, Bureau of Secondary School Supervision, to Mr. Benedict, State Education Department, University of the State of New York, dated Juky 14th, 1967.

[69] Earl Carldwell, Urban League plans Harlem Prep School, The New York Times, May 17, 1967

[70] Board of Regents, minutes, July 1967.

[71] Letter from Edward D. Loughman, Jr., to the Board of Regents, NY, June 13, 1967

[72] Report of Harlem Preparatory School, July 2, 1968

[73] Letter from Eugene S. Callender, NYUL, to Board of Regents, NY, June 7, 1967 .

[74] Maurice Carroll, "Harlem Dropouts head for College", The New York Times, Tuesday, October 3, 1967

[75] From materials provided by Harvey Spears October, 2014.

[76] Bruce Lambert, Edward F. Carpenter, 71, Is Dead; First Headmaster of Harlem Prep, January 9, 1992, New York Times; Unsung Hero Placed 164 Dropouts In College, NY Amsterdam News, Saturday, November 1st, 1969

[77] Edward F. Carpenter, the Development of an alternative school: Harlem Prep 1967-1972, PhD dissertation submitted to the University of Massachusetts School of Education, December, 1972.

[78] Harlem Prep application to the Board of Regents, July, 1967.

[79] From materials provided by Harvey Spears October, 2014.

[80] Marylin Bender, "For a benefit, the party may be casual, but the social commitment isn't", New York Times, November 23, 1971

[81] Vivian Perlis, Libby Van Cleve, Composer's voices from Ives to Ellington: an Oral History of American Music, (New Haven, CT: Yale U. Press, 2005) 404

[82] Carroll, "Harlem Dropouts head for College"

[83] Ibid.

[84] "I can do anything", Newsweek, July 8, 1968

[85] Ibid

[86] Homer Bigart, "Harlem Prep gives dropouts a Door to College", The New York Times, Wednesday, May 8, 1968

[87] Homer Bigart, "Harlem Prep gives dropouts a Door to College", The New York Times, Wednesday, May 8, 1968

[88] "I can do anything", Newsweek

[89] Report of Harlem Preparatory School, July 2, 1968, 2.

[90] Carroll, "Harlem Dropouts head for College"

[91] "I can do anything", Newsweek

[92] Carroll, "Harlem Dropouts head for College"

[93] Homer Bigart, "Harlem Prep gives dropouts a Door to College", The New York Times, Wednesday, May 8, 1968

[94] "I can do Anything', Newsweek

[95] Barnard L. Collier, "A Dropout Picks Up Some logic on His Way to College", The New York Times, Thursday, March 14, 1968

[96] "IBM Assists Special Summer Program", IBM News, Vol. 6, No. 16, August 25, 1969.

[97] Whitney M. Young Jr., "All a School Has To Do Is To Care", The Record, Tuesday, February 27, 1968

[98] Robert Mcg. Thomas Jr., 'Stephen Wright, 85; Led in Education for Blacks', the New York Times, April 19, 1996

[99] Dennison, George, The Lives of Children: The Story of the First Street School, (Random House Inc (P) (June 1970)) 9

[100] Preston R. Wilcox, "The community-centered school", Ronald and Beatrice Gross, Radical School Reform, (NY, NY: Simon and Schuster 1969) 127

[101] Kenneth Clark, "Ghetto Education: New Directions", Gross, Radical School Reform, 118

[102] Diane Ravitch, The Great School Wars: A history of the New York City public schools, (Baltimore, MD: Johns Hopkins U. Press, 2000) 290

[103] Wilcox, "The community-centered school" 129

[104] Ibid 126

[105] Herbert R. Kohl, The open classroom a practical guide to a new way of teaching, (NY, NY: New York Review Book, 1971) 12

[106] Ibid 13

[107] Dennison, The Lives of Children, 97

[108] (Kohl, The open classroom, 14)

[109] Ibid 19-20

[110] 20

[111] 31

[112] Dennison, The Lives of Children, 98

[113] Promotional material, Alen Scouten, project designer, Haase and Jackson architects

[114] Homer Bigart, "Harlem Prep gives dropouts a Door to College", The New York Times, Wednesday, May 8, 1968

[115] Harlem Prep promotional material, funded and published by the Standard Oil Company of New Jersey

[116] Description adapted from a booklet published by Haase and Jackson architects and Alan Scouten, Project Manager.

[117] Baha'u'llah, Gleanings from the Writings of Baha'u'llah, (Baha'i Publishing Trust: Wilmette, IL 1990) 259-260

[118] Daniel C. Jordan, Donald T. Streets, "The Anisa Model: A New Vision and a New Way in Early Education", In R. Blodget, A comprehensive paradigm of teaching (Dissertation). Cambridge, MA: University of Massachusetts. Retrieved February, 2015, from:
http://teach.valdosta.edu/anisa/blodget/anisa_new_vision1.pdf

[119] Annamarie Honnold, Vignettes from the Life of 'Abdu'l-Bahá, (Baha'i Trust: Wilmette, IL 1982) 139

[120] Statement by George "Sandy" Campbell http://mojalogo.blogspot.com/

[121] From biographical information provide by George "Sandy" Campbell

[122] From an interview with Cliff Jacobs.

[123] Standard Oil Company, Story of Harlem Preparatory School, 1969

[124] From interviews with Elizabeth McLoughlin

[125] From testimonials by the Czerniejewski family.

[126] "IBM Assists Special Summer Program", IBM News, Vol. 6, No. 16, August 25, 1969.

[127] "I can do anything", Newsweek

[128] "Unsung Hero Placed 164 Dropouts in College", Amsterdam News, Sat., Nov. 1, 1969.

[129] Ibid.

[130] Catherine Ross-Stroud, A Talk with Janet McDonald, The ALAN Review, Fall, 2009, http://scholar.lib.vt.edu/ejournals/ALAN/v37n1/pdf/ross.pdf

[131] Harlem Prep students, Cyril James, Ed., The Best of 40 Acres Poetry, (NY, NY: Horizon Six 1972)

[132] James, Ed., The Best of 40 Acres of Poetry, 10

[133] Ibid 7

[134] 12

[135] 13

[136] From a scrapbook of Harlem Prep memories provided by Liz McLoughlin

[137] Alberto O. Cappas, The Pledge, 1997

[138] John Mathews, "Storefront Academy Rescues Harlem Kids", The Evening Star, Thursday, Feb. 12, 1970

[139] Larry Cuban, How Teachers Taught: Constancy and Change in American Classrooms 1880-1990, (Teacher's College Press: NY, NY 1993) 175

[140] Diane Divoky, "New York's Mini-Schools", Saturday Review, December 18, 1971

[141] From an interview with Congressman Charles Rangel, January 10, 2015.

[142] Sonia Sanchez, "Hailu", retrieved October 10, 2014
http://www.afropoets.net/soniasanchez1.html

[143] Elijah Muhammad, (1965) Message to the Blackman in America, Muhammad's Temple No 2, ISBN 978-1-929594-01-6, p. 16-17.

[144] (Kozol 76-7)

[145] From interviews with Dwight Allen and Don Streets.

[146] (Kozol 111)

[147] Letter from Judge Robert Mangum November 1979

[148] C Gerald Fraser, "Harlem Prep Is Striving To Survive as Funds Fall", The new York Times, Monday, December 4, 1972

[149] Steve Duncan, "Harlem Prep Praised to Heavens, but Funding is Hell", Sunday Daily News, Sunday, April 26, 1970.

[150] "Harlem Prep and Street Academies Periled", New York Times, Tuesday, February 16, 1971.

[151] "Experiments Worth Saving", New York Times, Monday, February 22,1971

[152] "Blacks Remain Far Behind Whites in Most Categories, Census Data Show", The New York Times, Monday, July 23, 1973

[153] Bender, "For a benefit, the party may be casual, but the social commitment isn't",

[154] C. Gerald Fraser, "$250,000 Jersey Standard Gift Gives Harlem Prep a Reprieve", The New York Times, March 6, 1971

[155] Harlem Prep yearbook, 1970

[156] "Goings, Russell L. Jr.", retrieved December 2, 2014 http://www.encyclopedia.com/doc/1G2-2694400032.html

[157] New York Urban Coalition, "What's the big deal about min-school teacher, anyway? Who are they?", mini-school news, 4-5

[158] Ibid 4-5

[159] 4-5

[160] Milton Adams, "School for Dropouts May Have to Drop Out", New York Post, November 22, 1972, 31

[161] Ibid 31

[162] Committee to Save Harlem Prep, Fundraising letter, "Harlem Prep presents: An Evening with a Dream"

[163] Iver Peterson, "Take-Over by City Called Harlem Prep's Only Hope"< New York Times, Thursday, August 9, 1973

[164] Mary Kelly, "Harlem Prep shows fine results with dropouts but hits financial shoals", The Christian Science Monitor", Thursday, August 16, 1973

[165] Ibid

[166] Ibid

[167] James L. Hicks, "Another Angle", Amsterdam News, Saturday, September 15, 1973

[168] "Harlem Prep dies For Lack Of Funds", Amsterdan News, Saturday, September 15, 1973

[169] "Education: Vale, Harlem Prep", Time, Monday, October 1, 1973

[170] George Goodman Jr., "Take-Over Sought At Harlem Prep", The New York Times, November, 22, 1973

[171] Bernard Bard, "City's School System Absorbing Harlem Prep", New York Post, Wednesday, November 21st, 1973

[172] "Can Harlem Prep School Go It Alone", New York Post, Friday, December 7, 1973

[173] Ibid

[174] Lucile Davis, Malcolm X, (Bridgestone Books: Mankato. MN 1998) 22

[175] Institute of Education Services-National Center for Education Statistics, Alternative Schools and Programs for Public School Students at Risk of Educational Failure: 2007-2008 http://nces.ed.gov/pubs2010/2010026.pdf

[176] National Alliance for Charter Schools, The Public Charter Schools Dashboard, http://dashboard.publiccharters.org/dashboard/schools/page/overview/year/2011

[177] Christine H. Rossell, "Magnet Schools", Education Next, http://educationnext.org/magnetschools/

Notes

34030390R00082

Made in the USA
Middletown, DE
05 August 2016